TREASURY BONDS INVESTING 101

Build Long-Term Income with Government-Backed Bonds

Usiere Uko

ISBN-13: 979-8-853-58711-3

FIRST EDITION

...To new frontiers, learning and growing

CONTENTS

INTRODUCTION

A BEGINNER'S GUIDE TO LOW-RISK INVESTMENT STRATEGIES

Treasury Bonds investing welcomes not only Wall Street players, celebrities, and high net worth individuals but also individuals like you and me. It stands as a valuable tool, enabling you to cultivate a stable income by putting our money to work diligently. With Treasury Bonds, you can harness the power of compounding and foster financial growth for a prosperous future.

The journey of a thousand mile begins with a single step, according to a Chinese proverb. That's precisely what we're embarking on together - a journey toward building a solid and secure financial future. So, whether you're young or old, brand new to the world of investing or just looking to expand your knowledge, you've come to the right place.

In this book, we'll take you by the hand and walk you through the exciting realm of Treasury Bonds - government-backed securities that hold the promise of steady returns and low-risk investing. We'll break down the complex concepts into bite-sized pieces, so you can confidently navigate this fascinating world, no matter your prior experience.

We're all on a unique financial journey, and here, we embrace that diversity. Maybe you're dreaming of an early retirement on a tropical beach, funding your children's education, or simply ensuring a stable future for yourself and your loved ones. Whatever your goals may be, understanding Treasury Bonds and low-risk investment strategies can be a vital step toward achieving them.

As your trusted companion, we'll cover the fundamental questions: What exactly are Treasury Bonds, and how do they work? What are the benefits of investing in them, and what risks should we be mindful of? But we won't stop there. We'll venture further into the landscape of practical investment strategies, learning how to craft a diversified portfolio and safeguard against potential pitfalls.

Rest assured, this journey is about more than just facts and figures. It's about empowerment, confidence, and making well-informed decisions that align with your unique financial goals. We'll equip you with the tools you need to navigate the twists and turns of the investment world while maintaining a focus on security and steady growth.

Finance can be exciting and rewarding, and we'll show you how to embrace that excitement on your path to financial freedom.

So, are you ready to set sail into the world of Treasury Bonds and low-risk investment strategies? If you are, then turn the page and let's dive right in. We're about to embark on an enlightening journey that may just change the course of your financial future.

PART 1: INTRODUCTION TO TREASURY BONDS

1: WHAT ARE TREASURY BONDS?

L et's take a dive into the world of Treasury Bonds and get you acquainted with these essential investment instruments. At their core, Treasury Bonds are government debt securities issued by the U.S. Department of the Treasury.

These bonds serve as a way for the government to borrow money from investors, like you, to finance various projects and fund its operations. As an investor, when you purchase a Treasury Bond, you are effectively lending money to the U.S. government.

One of the most appealing aspects of Treasury Bonds is their reputation for being a low-risk investment. Why? Because they are backed by the full faith and credit of the United States government. This means that the chance of the government defaulting on its debt obligations is exceptionally low, making Treasury Bonds one of the safest investments available in the financial market.

Here are some key points to know about Treasury Bonds:

Fixed Interest Rate: When you invest in a Treasury Bond, you'll receive periodic interest payments, known as coupon payments, at a fixed interest rate. The interest rate is determined at the time of issuance and remains constant throughout the bond's life.

Maturity Period: Treasury Bonds have longer maturities compared to other types of government securities. They typically come in maturities of 10 years or more. At the end of the maturity period, the government will pay back the bond's face value, which is the initial amount you invested.

Predictable Income: The fixed interest payments provided by Treasury Bonds can offer a predictable income stream to investors. This makes them attractive to individuals seeking stability and consistent returns.

Liquidity: Treasury Bonds are highly liquid investments, meaning you can easily buy or sell them in the financial market. This flexibility allows you to adjust your investment strategy according to changing financial circumstances or personal goals.

Taxation: While the interest income earned from Treasury Bonds is subject to federal income tax, it is exempt from state and local taxes. This tax advantage can make Treasury Bonds even more appealing to certain investors, depending on their tax situation.

Diversification: Incorporating Treasury Bonds into your investment portfolio can help diversify your holdings and spread risk, as they often behave differently than stocks and other higher-risk investments.

As you progress through this guide, we'll explore the various aspects of Treasury Bonds in greater detail. You'll gain a deeper understanding of how they work, the different types available, their advantages, potential risks, and strategies for incorporating them effectively into your investment plan.

Whether you're a seasoned investor looking to expand your portfolio or a newcomer seeking to build a solid financial foundation, understanding Treasury Bonds is a crucial step towards achieving your financial goals. So, let's embark on this journey together and unlock the potential of Treasury Bonds as a valuable addition to your investment toolkit.

Let's move on to Chapter 2, where we'll delve into the world of government securities and further explore the landscape of Treasury Bonds.

2: UNDERSTANDING GOVERNMENT SECURITIES

Government securities are debt instruments issued by national governments to raise capital for various purposes, such as funding infrastructure projects, social programs, and budgetary needs. These securities play a crucial role in the global economy and are known for their stability and low-risk nature.

In this chapter, we'll take a closer look at government securities and their significance in the financial market.

GOVERNMENT DEBT AND ITS IMPORTANCE

Governments, like any other entity, may sometimes require funds beyond their immediate revenues. To bridge this gap, they issue debt in the form of government securities. These securities are essentially promises to repay the borrowed money along with interest over a specified period. Governments use the proceeds from the sale of these securities to finance public initiatives and keep their economies running smoothly.

TYPES OF GOVERNMENT SECURITIES

Government securities come in various forms, and each has unique characteristics. Some common types include Treasury Bills (T-Bills), Treasury Notes (T-Notes), Treasury Bonds (T-Bonds), and Treasury Inflation-Protected Securities (TIPS).

Among these, Treasury Bonds are long-term debt instruments with maturities typically ranging from 10 to 30 years.

SAFETY AND CREDIT RATING

One of the most attractive features of government securities, including Treasury Bonds, is their safety. Since they are backed by the government's ability to tax and its power to print money, the risk of default is minimal. As a result, government securities are often considered risk-free assets. Credit rating agencies assess government securities and assign credit ratings to them, providing investors with an idea of the government's creditworthiness.

ROLE IN MONETARY POLICY

Government securities play a critical role in the implementation of monetary policy by central banks. Central banks can influence the money supply and interest rates by buying or selling government securities in the open market. For example, when a central bank wants to increase the money supply, it buys government securities, injecting funds into the economy and lowering interest rates.

GLOBAL SIGNIFICANCE

Government securities, especially those issued by major economies, are considered benchmarks for global financial markets. Investors often view them as a safe haven during times of economic uncertainty or market volatility. Additionally, government securities serve as a reference point for pricing other debt instruments, such as corporate bonds.

SECONDARY MARKET TRADING

Government securities, including Treasury Bonds, are actively traded in the secondary market. After their initial issuance, investors can buy and sell these securities on various financial exchanges. The secondary market provides liquidity to investors, allowing them to adjust their portfolios according to changing market conditions or investment objectives.

As we progress through this guide, we'll focus primarily on Treasury Bonds and explore how they differ from other government securities. Understanding the unique features and benefits of Treasury Bonds will equip you with the knowledge needed to make informed investment decisions.

In the next chapter, we'll delve specifically into Treasury Bonds, their benefits, and how they can be a valuable addition to your investment portfolio.

3: BENEFITS OF INVESTING IN TREASURY BONDS

We'll now explore the numerous benefits that investing in Treasury Bonds can offer to both seasoned and novice investors alike. Treasury Bonds have been a preferred investment choice for generations, and for good reason. Let's dive into the advantages they bring to your financial journey:

SAFETY AND LOW RISK

One of the primary reasons investors flock to Treasury Bonds is their unparalleled safety. Backed by the U.S. government, these bonds are considered one of the safest investments in the world. The likelihood of the U.S. government defaulting on its debt obligations is extremely low, providing you with peace of mind and a secure foundation for your portfolio.

STABLE INCOME STREAM

Treasury Bonds offer a predictable income stream through their fixed interest payments, or coupon payments. These payments are made at regular intervals, typically semi-annually, and the interest rate remains constant throughout the bond's life. This stability can be particularly attractive for retirees or those seeking a reliable source of income.

DIVERSIFICATION AND RISK MANAGEMENT

Incorporating Treasury Bonds into your investment portfolio can significantly enhance diversification. Since Treasury Bonds often have a low correlation with other asset classes, such as stocks, they can help reduce overall portfolio risk. During times of market volatility or economic uncertainty, the stability of Treasury Bonds can act as a counterbalance to riskier investments.

CAPITAL PRESERVATION

The assurance of receiving the bond's face value at maturity offers capital preservation. As long as you hold the Treasury Bonds until it matures, you will receive the full face value of the bond back, regardless of fluctuations in interest rates or bond prices during its lifetime.

TAX ADVANTAGES

Interest income from Treasury Bonds is subject to federal income tax, but it is exempt from state and local taxes. This tax advantage can be especially valuable for investors in high-tax jurisdictions, as it helps optimize the after-tax returns on your investments.

LIQUIDITY AND FLEXIBILITY

Treasury Bonds are highly liquid, meaning you can easily buy or sell them in the secondary market before their maturity date. This liquidity provides you with the flexibility to adjust your investment strategy in response to changing financial conditions or personal goals.

PORTFOLIO HEDGING

Treasury Bonds can serve as an effective hedge against inflation and economic downturns. Inflation-indexed Treasury Bonds (TIPS) provide protection against rising inflation, as their principal and interest payments adjust with changes in the consumer price index (CPI). During economic downturns or stock market declines, Treasury Bonds often perform well as investors seek safer assets.

ACCESSIBLE TO INDIVIDUAL INVESTORS

Investing in Treasury Bonds is accessible to individual investors with various budget sizes. You can purchase Treasury Bonds directly from the government through the TreasuryDirect website or through brokerage accounts and financial institutions.

FAVORABLE FOR RETIREMENT PLANNING

For individuals planning for retirement, Treasury Bonds can play a vital role in creating a balanced and secure retirement portfolio. Their low risk and reliable income stream can help ensure a more stable financial future during retirement.

Overall, Treasury Bonds offer a unique combination of safety, stability, and income potential. They have stood the test of time as a go-to investment for risk-averse individuals, income-focused investors, and those seeking diversification in their portfolios.

In the next chapter, we will explore the potential risks associated with Treasury Bonds. Understanding both the benefits and risks will empower you to make well-informed investment decisions and design a strong financial foundation. Let's move forward and delve into Chapter 4, where we will address these risks in detail.

4: RISKS ASSOCIATED WITH TREASURY BONDS

While Treasury Bonds are widely regarded as safe and low-risk investments, like any financial instrument, they are not without their own set of risks. In this chapter, we'll explore the potential risks associated with investing in Treasury Bonds:

INTEREST RATE RISK

One of the primary risks facing Treasury Bonds investors is interest rate risk. As fixed-income securities, the prices of Treasury Bonds are sensitive to changes in interest rates. When interest rates rise, newly issued bonds offer higher yields, making existing bonds with lower fixed rates less attractive to investors. As a result, the market value of existing Treasury Bonds may decrease, especially those with longer maturities. Conversely, when interest rates decline, the market value of existing bonds may increase.

INFLATION RISK

While Treasury Bonds are considered safer than many other investments, they are not immune to inflation risk. Inflation erodes the purchasing power of fixed-interest payments over time. Although Treasury Bonds pay a fixed interest rate, their real returns (adjusted for inflation) may decrease if the inflation rate surpasses the bond's interest rate. To mitigate inflation risk, investors can consider Treasury Inflation-Protected Securities (TIPS), which adjust their principal and interest payments with changes in the inflation rate.

OPPORTUNITY COST

Investing in Treasury Bonds, particularly those with longer maturities, ties up your funds for a specific period. During this time, you may miss out on potentially higher returns from other investments, such as stocks or riskier bonds. While the stability of Treasury Bonds can be beneficial, it's essential to consider your overall investment strategy and the opportunity cost of allocating a significant portion of your portfolio to lower-yield, fixed-income assets.

CALL RISK (FOR CALLABLE BONDS)

Some Treasury Bonds, known as callable bonds, come with call provisions that allow the government to redeem the bonds before their scheduled maturity date. If interest rates decline significantly, the government may choose to call the bonds to refinance its debt at a lower cost. This can result in an early return of principal to the investor, leaving them with the task of reinvesting the proceeds at potentially lower interest rates.

CREDIT RISK (FOR NON-U.S. GOVERNMENT BONDS)

While U.S. Treasury Bonds are considered virtually free of credit risk due to the government's strong creditworthiness, the same may not be true for bonds issued by other governments. Investing in foreign government bonds introduces credit risk, which refers to the possibility of the issuer defaulting on its debt obligations. Investors need to be cautious when considering non-U.S. government bonds and assess the creditworthiness of the issuing country.

MARKET RISK

Market risk affects all investments and reflects the potential for the overall financial markets to experience volatility. Changes in economic conditions, geopolitical events, or shifts in investor sentiment can influence the prices of Treasury Bonds and lead to fluctuations in their market values.

REINVESTMENT RISK

For investors who rely on the income from Treasury Bonds, there is a reinvestment risk. When the bond's interest payments are received, investors may face challenges finding similarly attractive investment opportunities to reinvest the funds at comparable interest rates, especially during periods of declining interest rates.

While these risks should be taken into consideration, it's important to recognize that the level of risk associated with Treasury Bonds is relatively lower compared to many other investments. The U.S. government's commitment to repaying its debt and the backing of the full faith and credit of the nation provide a significant level of security.

As an investor, it's crucial to weigh the potential risks against the benefits of investing in Treasury Bonds and align your investment strategy with your financial goals, risk tolerance, and time horizon. Understanding the risks will empower you to make well-informed decisions and build a balanced investment portfolio.

In the next part of this guide, we'll explore the various types of Treasury Bonds available, allowing you to gain a deeper understanding of the options at your disposal as you build a solid investment portfolio. Let's move forward to Part 2: Types of Treasury Bonds.

PART 2: TYPES OF TREASURY BONDS

5: FIXED-RATE VS. INFLATION-INDEXED TREASURY BONDS

In this chapter, we will explore the key differences between fixed-rate and inflation-indexed Treasury Bonds, shedding light on their unique characteristics and the benefits they offer to investors. Each type of bond presents distinct advantages, catering to different investment goals and economic circumstances.

FIXED-RATE TREASURY BONDS

Fixed-rate Treasury Bonds, also known as nominal Treasury Bonds, offer a consistent and predetermined interest rate throughout their term. When you invest in a fixed-rate Treasury Bonds, you lock in a specific interest rate at the time of purchase, and this rate remains unchanged over the life of the bond. As a result, fixed-rate bonds provide a predictable income stream to investors through semi-annual interest payments.

BENEFITS OF FIXED-RATE TREASURY BONDS:

Stability and Predictability: Fixed-rate Treasury Bonds are favored by risk-averse investors seeking stability and a reliable income source. The fixed interest payments offer consistent returns regardless of fluctuations in interest rates or changes in the broader economic environment.

Cash Flow Management: The predictable income stream from fixed-rate bonds makes them valuable for individuals who depend on regular interest payments to manage their cash flow needs, especially during retirement.

Long-Term Investment Planning: Investors with specific long-term financial goals can benefit from fixed-rate Treasury Bonds, as they allow for more precise financial planning due to the predictable nature of the bond's cash flows.

INFLATION-INDEXED TREASURY BONDS (TIPS)

Inflation-Indexed Treasury Bonds, or Treasury Inflation-Protected Securities (TIPS), are designed to protect investors against the erosive effects of inflation. Unlike fixed-rate bonds, the principal value of TIPS adjusts with changes in the Consumer Price Index for All Urban Consumers (CPI-U). Additionally, the semi-annual interest payments are based on the inflation-adjusted principal, providing investors with a real rate of return.

BENEFITS OF INFLATION-INDEXED TREASURY BONDS (TIPS):

Inflation Protection: TIPS shield investors from the eroding impact of inflation. As consumer prices rise, the principal value of the bond increases, and subsequently, the interest payments rise as well. This ensures that the purchasing power of the bondholder remains relatively stable over time.

Preservation of Capital: With the inflation adjustment, the risk of seeing the real value of the investment diminish due to rising prices is significantly reduced. Investors can have confidence in the preservation of their capital in real terms.

Diversification and Hedging: TIPS provide a unique diversification opportunity in a portfolio, particularly during periods of rising inflation. Their performance often differs from that of other asset classes, making them a valuable hedge against inflationary pressures.

CHOOSING THE RIGHT BOND FOR YOUR PORTFOLIO

Deciding between fixed-rate and inflation-indexed Treasury

Bonds depends on your investment objectives, risk tolerance, and the prevailing economic conditions. If you seek stable income and cash flow predictability, fixed-rate Treasury Bonds may be more suitable. On the other hand, if you are concerned about the impact of inflation on your investments and wish to protect your purchasing power, inflation-indexed Treasury Bonds (TIPS) offer a valuable solution.

Both types of Treasury Bonds can play complementary roles in a diversified investment portfolio. Combining fixed-rate and inflation-indexed bonds allows you to create a well-rounded strategy that addresses both income needs and inflation protection.

As you continue your journey in Treasury Bond investing, understanding the benefits of each type of bond will help you craft a robust and adaptable portfolio that aligns with your financial aspirations and safeguards your wealth in varying economic environments.

Let's move forward to Chapter 6, where we'll explore the differences between Treasury Notes, Treasury Bonds, and Treasury Bills, allowing you to broaden your understanding of the diverse offerings in the world of government securities.

6: TREASURY NOTES VS. TREASURY BONDS VS. TREASURY BILLS

L et's examine the key differences among three essential types of government securities: Treasury Notes, Treasury Bonds, and Treasury Bills. Each of these instruments serves a specific purpose in the financial market, and understanding their unique features will help you navigate the world of government securities more effectively.

TREASURY NOTES

Treasury Notes, commonly referred to as T-Notes, are medium-term government securities with maturities ranging from 2 to 10 years. They pay semi-annual interest to bondholders at a fixed coupon rate. T-Notes strike a balance between short-term liquidity and long-term investment potential, making them attractive to investors seeking a steady income stream with a moderate time commitment.

Key Characteristics of Treasury Notes:

- **Medium-Term Maturity**: 2 to 10 years.

- **Fixed Coupon Rate**: Pays semi-annual interest at a predetermined rate.

- **Steady Income Stream**: Provides investors with predictable interest payments over the bond's term.

TREASURY BONDS

Treasury Bonds, also known as T-Bonds, are long-term government securities with maturities typically ranging from 10 to 30 years. Like Treasury Notes, they pay semi-annual interest to bond-holders at a fixed coupon rate. T-Bonds appeal to investors with long investment horizons and those seeking a reliable income source with a focus on capital preservation.

Key Characteristics of Treasury Bonds:

- **Long-Term Maturity:** 10 to 30 years.

- **Fixed Coupon Rate**: Pays semi-annual interest at a predetermined rate.

- **Reliable Income**: Provides a stable income stream over the bond's extended life.

TREASURY BILLS

Treasury Bills, often referred to as T-Bills, are short-term government securities with maturities of one year or less. Unlike Treasury Notes and Treasury Bonds, T-Bills do not pay periodic interest (coupon payments). Instead, they are issued at a discount to their face value and redeemed at full face value upon maturity, effectively providing interest through the difference between the purchase price and the face value.

Key Characteristics of Treasury Bills:

- **Short-Term Maturity**: One year or less.

- **Discount Issuance**: Sold at a price below the face value, with the difference representing the interest earned.

- **Liquidity and Cash Management:** T-Bills are highly liquid and serve as a safe haven for short-term funds.

CHOOSING THE RIGHT GOVERNMENT SECURITY

Deciding between Treasury Notes, Treasury Bonds, and Treasury

Bills depends on your investment goals, risk appetite, and time horizon. If you prioritize steady income with moderate time commitments, Treasury Notes and Treasury Bonds may suit your needs. Conversely, if you seek a safe and highly liquid place for short-term funds, Treasury Bills provide an optimal solution.

Many investors opt to include a mix of these government securities in their portfolio, benefiting from the unique advantages each type offers. This diversification allows for greater adaptability to varying market conditions and aligns with individual financial objectives.

As you explore the world of government securities, understanding the differences among Treasury Notes, Treasury Bonds, and Treasury Bills will aid you in constructing a well-balanced investment portfolio that aligns with your financial aspirations and risk tolerance.

In the next chapter, we'll delve into the issuance and auction process of Treasury Bonds, providing insights into how these securities are introduced to the market. Let's proceed to Chapter 7: Issuance and Auction Process.

PART 3: HOW TREASURY BONDS WORK

7: ISSUANCE AND AUCTION PROCESS

I n this chapter, we'll delve into the issuance and auction process of Treasury Bonds, providing valuable insights into how these essential government securities are introduced to the market. By understanding the issuance and auction process of Treasury Bonds, investors can grasp the mechanisms through which these vital government securities are made available to the public.

ISSUANCE OF TREASURY BONDS

The U.S. Department of the Treasury is responsible for issuing Treasury Bonds. The Treasury determines the timing, maturities, and the total amount of bonds to be issued based on the government's funding needs and debt management strategy.

PRIMARY DEALERS

To facilitate the sale of Treasury Bonds, the Treasury works with a group of financial institutions known as primary dealers. These primary dealers, typically large banks and securities firms, participate in the auction process and serve as intermediaries between the Treasury and the secondary market where the bonds are traded.

AUCTION PROCESS

The primary method of selling Treasury Bonds is through auctions. Treasury Bond auctions are held regularly, with specific schedules announced by the Treasury. The most common auction types are the competitive and non-competitive auctions.

COMPETITIVE AUCTION

In a competitive auction, institutional investors, such as banks and large financial institutions, submit bids indicating the quantity of bonds they wish to purchase and the yield (interest rate) they are willing to accept. Bids are ranked from the highest yield (lowest price) to the lowest yield (highest price).

NON-COMPETITIVE AUCTION

Individual investors typically participate in non-competitive auctions. In this type of auction, participants submit bids without specifying a particular yield. Instead, they agree to accept the yield determined by the competitive auction results.

AWARDING OF BONDS

The Treasury first awards the bonds to the highest bidder in the competitive auction, followed by successive awards to the next highest bidders until the entire offering is allocated. Non-competitive bidders receive the full amount of bonds they requested at the yield determined by the competitive auction.

SETTLEMENT AND DELIVERY

After the auction, successful bidders make payment for the purchased bonds through their respective custodial accounts at the Federal Reserve. The Treasury Bonds are then delivered to the investors' accounts, and interest payments begin in accordance with the bond's terms.

AFTERMARKET TRADING

Once issued, Treasury Bonds are actively traded in the secondary market. Investors can buy or sell these bonds at prevailing market prices, providing ample liquidity and flexibility for investors looking to adjust their bond holdings.

TREASURYDIRECT

Individual investors can also purchase Treasury Bonds directly from the government through the TreasuryDirect website. TreasuryDirect allows individuals to buy, manage, and redeem Treasury securities online without going through a broker or financial intermediary.

Participating in Treasury Bond auctions or using TreasuryDirect offers investors direct access to these safe and reliable investments. In the next chapter, we'll explore the concept of interest payments and coupon rates, providing insights into how investors receive returns from their Treasury Bond investments. Let's proceed to Chapter 8: Interest Payments and Coupon Rates.

8: INTEREST PAYMENTS AND COUPON RATES

U nderstanding how interest payments and coupon rates associated with Treasury Bonds work is crucial for investors seeking steady income and reliable returns from their bond investments. It empowers you to make informed investment decisions and align your bond investments with your financial goals.

COUPON RATE EXPLAINED

The coupon rate of a Treasury Bond represents the fixed annual interest rate paid to the bondholder. When you purchase a Treasury Bond, you lock in this coupon rate, and it remains constant throughout the bond's life.

For example, if a Treasury Bond has a coupon rate of 3%, and its face value is $1,000, you will receive annual interest payments of $30 (3% of $1,000) over the bond's term.

FIXED INTEREST PAYMENTS

The coupon payments on Treasury Bonds are typically made semi-annually. For a bond with a face value of $1,000 and a 3% coupon rate, you would receive two payments of $15 each over the year. These regular interest payments provide a steady income stream to investors, making Treasury Bonds an attractive option for those seeking reliable returns.

CALCULATION OF INTEREST PAYMENTS

To calculate the interest payment for a specific period, simply multiply the face value of the bond by the coupon rate and divide by the number of interest payments per year.

For instance, a $1,000 Treasury Bond with a 2.5% coupon rate will have semi-annual interest payments of $12.50 each ($1,000 x 2.5% ÷ 2).

RELATIONSHIP BETWEEN COUPON RATE AND MARKET INTEREST RATES

The coupon rate of a Treasury Bond is determined at the time of issuance and remains fixed. However, the bond's market price may fluctuate in response to changes in prevailing interest rates. If the bond's coupon rate is higher than current market interest rates, it becomes more attractive to investors, and its price may rise above the face value. Conversely, if the coupon rate is lower than prevailing rates, the bond's price may fall below its face value.

REINVESTMENT RISK AND COUPON RATES

Another important consideration for investors is reinvestment risk. This risk arises from the possibility that when interest payments are received, investors may not be able to reinvest those funds at the same coupon rate. If prevailing interest rates are lower, reinvesting the interest income may result in lower returns.

ZERO-COUPON TREASURY BONDS

In addition to regular Treasury Bonds with fixed coupon rates, the U.S. Treasury also issues zero-coupon Treasury Bonds. These bonds do not make periodic interest payments but are instead sold at a discount to their face value. The investor receives the full face value of the bond at maturity, effectively earning the difference between the purchase price and the face value as interest.

In the next chapter, we'll explore the process of calculating yield and returns on Treasury Bonds, allowing you to assess the overall performance of your bond investments. Let's move on to Chapter 9: Calculating Yield and Returns.

9: CALCULATING YIELD AND RETURNS

L et's explore the essential concepts of calculating yield and returns on Treasury Bonds. Understanding how to evaluate the performance of your bond investments is crucial for making informed decisions and assessing the overall effectiveness of your portfolio.

YIELD TO MATURITY (YTM)

Yield to Maturity (YTM) is a critical metric for measuring the total return an investor can expect to earn if they hold a Treasury Bond until its maturity. YTM takes into account the bond's current market price, its face value, the time remaining until maturity, and the coupon rate. It represents the average annual return the investor will achieve if all interest payments are reinvested at the same yield until the bond matures.

CALCULATING YTM

While the YTM calculation involves complex mathematical formulas, it can be easily determined using financial calculators or online tools. It's essential to remember that YTM assumes all interest payments are reinvested at the same rate, which may not be practical in reality due to changing interest rate conditions.

CURRENT YIELD

Current Yield is a simplified measure of a bond's return, calculated by dividing the annual interest (coupon) payment by the bond's current market price. Unlike YTM, Current Yield does not take into account the bond's time to maturity or the effect of reinvesting interest payments.

PRICE AND YIELD RELATIONSHIP

The price of a Treasury Bond and its yield have an inverse relationship. When market interest rates rise, newly issued bonds offer higher coupon rates, making existing bonds with lower fixed coupon rates less attractive. As a result, the market price of existing bonds falls to make them competitive with new issuances. Conversely, when market interest rates fall, existing bonds become more desirable, driving their prices up.

REALIZED YIELD

Realized Yield is the actual return an investor achieves over the holding period of the bond, taking into account any changes in the bond's price and interest income received. It is the yield an investor experiences in practice, considering both interest payments and any capital gains or losses if the bond is sold before maturity.

REINVESTMENT RISK AND YIELD

Reinvestment risk is a significant consideration when calculating yield and returns. It arises from the uncertainty of reinvesting interest income at the same yield as the original investment. If market interest rates decline, the investor may face challenges in finding comparable reinvestment opportunities, potentially leading to a lower realized yield.

TOTAL RETURN

The Total Return of a Treasury Bond investment includes both interest income and any capital appreciation or depreciation over the holding period. It provides a comprehensive view of the bond's performance, accounting for all sources of return.

In the next part of this guide, we'll explore the advantages of Treasury Bonds as a low-risk investment, highlighting the benefits they offer to investors seeking stability and income potential. Let's move forward to Part 4: Advantages and Disadvantages.

PART 4: ADVANTAGES AND DISADVANTAGES

10: ADVANTAGES OF TREASURY BONDS AS A LOW-RISK INVESTMENT

There are numerous advantages that Treasury Bonds offer as a low-risk investment. Treasury Bonds, backed by the full faith and credit of the U.S. government, are considered one of the safest assets in the financial markets. As such, they play a vital role in providing stability and income potential for investors seeking to preserve capital and mitigate risk.

SAFETY AND SECURITY

One of the primary advantages of investing in Treasury Bonds is the unparalleled safety and security they provide. As obligations of the U.S. government, Treasury Bonds are backed by the nation's financial strength and ability to tax and raise revenue. This assurance of repayment makes them virtually free of credit risk, offering investors peace of mind in uncertain economic environments.

LOW CREDIT RISK

Unlike corporate bonds or other debt instruments, Treasury Bonds carry minimal credit risk. The U.S. government has a long-standing history of meeting its debt obligations and has never defaulted on its debt payments. This low credit risk is particularly appealing to risk-averse investors seeking a safe haven for their capital.

STEADY INCOME STREAM

With fixed coupon payments, Treasury Bonds provide a reliable and predictable income stream to investors. Whether you hold short-term, medium-term, or long-term Treasury Bonds, you can count on regular interest payments, making them an attractive option for individuals who rely on income to support their financial needs.

DIVERSIFICATION AND PORTFOLIO STABILITY

Treasury Bonds act as a diversification tool in an investment portfolio. When combined with other asset classes, such as stocks, corporate bonds, or real estate, Treasury Bonds can help reduce overall portfolio volatility and enhance stability during times of market turbulence.

HEDGE AGAINST MARKET VOLATILITY

During periods of economic uncertainty or market volatility, Treasury Bonds often serve as a hedge. Investors flock to these safe-haven assets, driving up their prices and lowering yields. As a result, holding Treasury Bonds can mitigate losses in other riskier investments, providing a cushion during market downturns.

INFLATION PROTECTION (for Inflation-Indexed Bonds)

Investors concerned about inflation can benefit from Treasury Inflation-Protected Securities (TIPS). These bonds provide a built-in hedge against rising inflation, as their principal and interest payments adjust with changes in the CPI-U, safeguarding the purchasing power of the bondholder.

LIQUIDITY AND ACCESSIBILITY

Treasury Bonds are highly liquid and actively traded in the secondary market. Investors can buy and sell these bonds with ease, allowing them to access their funds whenever needed without significant price fluctuations.

TAX ADVANTAGES

Interest income from Treasury Bonds is exempt from state and local taxes, offering potential tax advantages for investors, especially those residing in high-tax states.

Given the host of advantages they offer, Treasury Bonds are a favored choice for conservative investors seeking a stable and low-risk component in their investment portfolio. The next chapter will explore potential drawbacks and limitations of investing in Treasury Bonds, providing a well-rounded perspective on these government securities. Let's proceed to Chapter 11: Potential Drawbacks and Limitations.

11: POTENTIAL DRAWBACKS AND LIMITATIONS

There are potential drawbacks and limitations associated with investing in Treasury Bonds. While Treasury Bonds are widely regarded as low-risk investments, they may not be suitable for every investor or every market condition. Understanding these limitations will help you make well-informed decisions and create a balanced investment strategy that aligns with your financial goals.

LOWER RETURNS COMPARED TO RISKIER ASSETS

While Treasury Bonds provide stability and safety, they typically offer lower returns compared to riskier assets like stocks or corporate bonds. During periods of economic growth and rising interest rates, investors may find that other investments outperform Treasury Bonds in terms of yield.

INFLATION RISK FOR FIXED-RATE BONDS

Fixed-rate Treasury Bonds are vulnerable to inflation risk, especially during times of rising consumer prices. As inflation erodes the purchasing power of future interest payments and the bond's face value, investors may experience a decrease in the real value of their returns.

INTEREST RATE SENSITIVITY

All types of Treasury Bonds are sensitive to changes in interest rates. When market interest rates rise, the prices of existing bonds may decline, potentially leading to capital losses for investors who sell their bonds before maturity. Longer-term Treasury Bonds are particularly sensitive to interest rate fluctuations.

MARKET RISK

Although Treasury Bonds are considered safe from credit risk, they are not immune to general market risk. Economic conditions, geopolitical events, and changes in investor sentiment can influence the demand for Treasury Bonds and impact their prices in the secondary market.

OPPORTUNITY COST

Investing in Treasury Bonds may involve an opportunity cost, as allocating a significant portion of your portfolio to low-yield assets might limit your exposure to potentially higher-return investments in other asset classes.

LACK OF LIQUIDITY FOR LARGE INVESTMENTS

While Treasury Bonds are generally highly liquid, investors with substantial holdings may face limited liquidity, especially in the secondary market for less frequently traded bonds.

POTENTIAL FOR NEGATIVE REAL RETURNS (for Inflation-Indexed Bonds)

Although Treasury Inflation-Protected Securities (TIPS) offer protection against inflation, they are not immune to negative real returns if the rate of inflation exceeds the bond's yield.

HOLDING PERIOD AND MATURITY CONSTRAINTS

Investors who require liquidity in the short term may face constraints with Treasury Bonds, especially if they invest in long-term maturities. Selling Treasury Bonds before their maturity may result in potential capital gains or losses.

CONCENTRATION RISK

Investing heavily in a single asset class, such as Treasury Bonds, may lead to concentration risk. Diversification across different asset classes can help mitigate this risk.

TAX TREATMENT FOR INFLATION-INDEXED BONDS

While interest income from Treasury Bonds is exempt from state and local taxes, the inflation adjustments for TIPS are subject to federal income tax, potentially affecting the net returns for some investors.

Treasury Bonds serve as valuable components of a diversified investment portfolio, but investors should carefully weigh these limitations against the benefits they offer. In the next part of this guide, we'll explore ways to assess your financial goals and risk tolerance, helping you tailor your investment strategy to suit your individual needs. Let's proceed to Part 5: Assessing Your Financial Goals and Risk Tolerance.

PART 5: ASSESSING YOUR FINANCIAL GOALS AND RISK TOLERANCE

13: UNDERSTANDING YOUR INVESTMENT OBJECTIVES

I dentifying clear and well-defined financial goals is the foundation for creating a successful and tailored investment strategy. Whether you're investing in Treasury Bonds or any other asset class, aligning your investments with your objectives is essential for achieving long-term financial success.

DEFINING YOUR FINANCIAL GOALS

Begin by defining your financial goals, both short-term and long-term. Common objectives may include saving for retirement, funding education expenses, purchasing a home, or building an emergency fund. Each goal comes with its unique timeline and risk tolerance.

RISK TOLERANCE ASSESSMENT

Understanding your risk tolerance is vital in crafting an appropriate investment strategy. Evaluate your ability to withstand market fluctuations and your willingness to take on risk in pursuit of higher returns. Treasury Bonds are considered low-risk, but you may also consider other asset classes based on your risk tolerance.

TIME HORIZON

Consider the time horizon for each of your financial goals. Short-term goals, such as a vacation or emergency fund, may require investments with higher liquidity and stability, while long-term goals, like retirement, can tolerate more extended investment periods with potentially higher returns.

INCOME NEEDS

Assess your income needs and determine how your investments can help meet them. If you rely on investment income to cover expenses, you may seek a stable income stream from assets like Treasury Bonds.

GROWTH VS. INCOME

Decide whether your primary objective is capital growth or income generation. Treasury Bonds, known for steady income, are more suited to investors seeking income, while other asset classes like stocks may offer higher growth potential.

ASSET ALLOCATION

After defining your goals and risk tolerance, design an appropriate asset allocation strategy. Diversify your portfolio across various asset classes, including Treasury Bonds, to balance risk and return potential.

REVIEW AND ADJUST

As your life circumstances and financial goals evolve, regularly review and adjust your investment objectives and portfolio. Reassess your risk tolerance, time horizon, and financial goals periodically to ensure your investments remain aligned with your changing needs.

PROFESSIONAL GUIDANCE

Seeking professional financial advice can provide valuable insights and assistance in aligning your investment objectives with your overall financial plan. Financial advisors can help craft a personalized strategy tailored to your unique situation.

Understanding your investment objectives is a critical step in building a successful investment plan. With clear goals and a solid understanding of your risk tolerance, you can construct a well-balanced portfolio that incorporates low-risk assets like Treasury Bonds and other suitable investments.

In the next chapter, we'll explore how to evaluate your risk tolerance further, allowing you to make informed decisions about your asset allocation. Let's move on to Chapter 13: Evaluating Your Risk Tolerance.

13: EVALUATING YOUR RISK TOLERANCE

Evaluating your risk tolerance is an essential step in designing an investment strategy that aligns with your comfort level and financial goals. This is within the context of selling or buying treasury bonds in the secondary market, which is subject to price fluctuations due to the interplay of the forces of interest rates, inflation, demand and supply etc.

Assessing your risk tolerance helps you strike the right balance between risk and reward, ensuring that your investment approach is in harmony with your individual preferences and circumstances.

UNDERSTANDING RISK TOLERANCE

Risk tolerance refers to your willingness and ability to withstand fluctuations in the value of your investments. It involves assessing how comfortable you are with the possibility of both gains and losses in your portfolio.

RISK CAPACITY VS. RISK ATTITUDE

Risk tolerance comprises two main aspects: risk capacity and risk attitude. Risk capacity refers to your financial ability to bear losses without compromising your financial well-being. Risk attitude, on the other hand, relates to your emotional response to market volatility and the potential for investment gains or losses.

INVESTMENT TIME HORIZON

Your investment time horizon is a critical factor in determining your risk tolerance. Longer investment horizons may allow you to weather short-term market volatility and potentially take on more risk for the potential of higher returns.

ASSESSING YOUR COMFORT LEVEL

Consider how you feel during periods of market turbulence or when your investments experience fluctuations. If the idea of significant short-term losses makes you anxious or leads you to make impulsive decisions, you may have a lower risk tolerance.

RISK TOLERANCE QUESTIONNAIRES

Various risk tolerance questionnaires and tools are available online and through financial advisors. These tools help quantify your risk tolerance by asking questions about your financial situation, investment goals, and attitudes towards risk.

INVESTMENT EXPERIENCE

Your past experiences with investments and exposure to different asset classes can influence your risk tolerance. If you have experienced significant losses in the past, you may be more cautious in your risk-taking.

DIVERSIFICATION AND RISK MITIGATION

Diversification, spreading your investments across different asset classes, can help mitigate risk. A well-diversified portfolio can be tailored to match your risk tolerance while still pursuing your financial goals.

REGULAR REASSESSMENT

Your risk tolerance is not static and may evolve over time. Changes in personal circumstances, market conditions, or investment performance may necessitate a reassessment of your risk tolerance periodically.

BALANCING RISK AND REWARD

Evaluating your risk tolerance is about finding the right balance between risk and reward. It's essential to be honest with yourself about your comfort level and not to take on more risk than you can handle.

By aligning your risk tolerance with your investment objectives, you can construct a well-diversified portfolio that maximizes potential returns while still providing a level of comfort during market fluctuations. In the next part of this guide, we'll explore portfolio diversification and asset allocation, crucial elements in managing risk and optimizing your investment outcomes. Let's move forward to Part 6: Building a Treasury Bond Portfolio.

PART 6: BUILDING A TREASURY BOND PORTFOLIO

14: DIVERSIFICATION AND ASSET ALLOCATION

I n this chapter, we'll explore the fundamental concepts of diversification and asset allocation, key pillars of sound investment strategies. Understanding how to diversify your portfolio and allocate assets effectively can help you manage risk and optimize your investment returns.

DIVERSIFICATION: THE POWER OF SPREADING RISK

Diversification involves spreading your investments across different asset classes, industries, and geographic regions. The goal is to reduce the impact of individual asset performance on your overall portfolio. By holding a mix of assets with low correlation to one another, you can potentially cushion losses from underperforming assets with gains from others.

THE ROLE OF TREASURY BONDS IN DIVERSIFICATION

Treasury Bonds play a crucial role in diversification due to their low correlation with riskier assets like stocks. During periods of economic uncertainty or market downturns, Treasury Bonds tend to perform well, offsetting potential losses in other parts of the portfolio. As a result, they can act as a stabilizing force and reduce overall portfolio volatility.

ASSET ALLOCATION: TAILORING YOUR PORTFOLIO

Asset allocation involves determining the optimal mix of assets in your portfolio based on your risk tolerance, investment objectives, and time horizon. The main asset classes typically include stocks, bonds (including Treasury Bonds), cash, and real estate.

BALANCING RISK AND RETURN

The allocation between different asset classes is a delicate balance between risk and return. Generally, riskier assets like stocks have higher potential returns but also carry higher volatility and risk. On the other hand, bonds, especially Treasury Bonds, offer lower but more stable returns with reduced risk.

RISK TOLERANCE AND ASSET ALLOCATION

Your risk tolerance plays a significant role in asset allocation. If you have a higher risk tolerance, you may allocate a larger portion of your portfolio to stocks, while a lower risk tolerance may lead to a higher allocation to bonds, including Treasury Bonds.

REBALANCING: MAINTAINING YOUR TARGET ALLOCATION

Over time, as asset classes perform differently, your portfolio's allocation may deviate from your target allocation. Periodically rebalancing your portfolio brings it back in line with your desired asset allocation. Rebalancing typically involves selling over performing assets and buying underperforming ones.

DIVERSIFICATION BENEFITS AND LIMITATIONS

While diversification can reduce risk, it does not guarantee protection against all market fluctuations or losses. A highly diversified portfolio may still experience losses during significant market downturns. Additionally, over-diversification can dilute potential returns and make it challenging to track portfolio performance effectively.

CONSIDER YOUR FINANCIAL GOALS

Your investment objectives should guide your asset allocation decisions. Short-term goals may require a more conservative allocation with a higher proportion of fixed-income assets like Treasury Bonds, while long-term goals may tolerate a more aggressive allocation with greater exposure to growth assets like stocks.

PROFESSIONAL GUIDANCE

Seeking advice from a financial advisor can be invaluable in determining the most suitable asset allocation for your specific circumstances and financial goals.

Diversification and asset allocation are powerful tools for managing risk and optimizing investment outcomes. By incorporating Treasury Bonds into a diversified portfolio, investors can enhance stability and reduce overall volatility, especially during uncertain market conditions.

In the next chapter, we'll explore in-depth strategies for building a Treasury Bond portfolio, considering different investment horizons and risk profiles. Let's proceed to Chapter 15: Determining the Right Mix of Treasury Bonds.

15: DETERMINING THE RIGHT MIX OF TREASURY BONDS

The right allocation of Treasury Bonds depends on your unique financial goals, risk tolerance, and investment time horizon. By understanding the different types of Treasury Bonds and their characteristics, you can tailor your portfolio to suit your needs.

UNDERSTANDING TREASURY BOND TYPES

As discussed earlier, Treasury Bonds come in various maturities, including short-term, medium-term, and long-term. Each type offers distinct benefits and risks. Short-term Treasury Bonds provide more immediate liquidity, while long-term Treasury Bonds offer the potential for higher returns over extended periods.

MATCHING YOUR TIME HORIZON

Align the maturity of your Treasury Bonds with your investment time horizon. For short-term financial goals, consider investing in Treasury Bills or short-term Treasury Notes. For long-term goals, like retirement planning, long-term Treasury Bonds may offer more significant growth potential.

BALANCING RISK AND RETURN

Determine your risk tolerance and appetite for return. While longer-term Treasury Bonds generally offer higher yields, they are also more sensitive to interest rate changes. If you have a lower risk tolerance, a mix of short and medium-term Treasury Bonds might be more suitable.

CONSIDERING INFLATION PROTECTION

If protecting your investments from inflation is a priority, Treasury Inflation-Protected Securities (TIPS) could be a valuable addition to your portfolio. TIPS adjust their principal value with changes in the Consumer Price Index, offering a hedge against rising inflation.

DIVERSIFICATION WITHIN TREASURY BONDS

Even within the category of Treasury Bonds, diversification is essential. Consider investing in bonds with different maturities and coupon rates to create a well-rounded Treasury Bond portfolio.

ASSESSING YOUR INCOME NEEDS

If you rely on investment income to cover living expenses, focus on Treasury Bonds with coupon payments that align with your income needs. Semi-annual interest payments from Treasury Notes and Treasury Bonds can provide a steady income stream.

REBALANCING AND PERIODIC REVIEW

Regularly review your Treasury Bond portfolio to ensure it remains aligned with your financial goals and risk tolerance. Rebalancing can be necessary to maintain your desired asset allocation and adapt to changing market conditions.

PROFESSIONAL ADVICE

Consider seeking advice from a financial advisor who can help analyze your specific financial situation, provide tailored recommendations, and ensure your Treasury Bond portfolio aligns with your broader investment plan.

TAX CONSIDERATIONS

Be aware of the tax implications of your Treasury Bond investments. While Treasury Bond interest is exempt from state and local taxes, interest income is subject to federal income tax.

Determining the right mix of Treasury Bonds in your portfolio requires a careful evaluation of your financial goals, risk tolerance, and investment preferences. By creating a well-balanced Treasury Bond portfolio, you can enjoy the benefits of stability, reliable income, and potential growth that these government securities offer.

In the next part of this guide, we'll explore the various methods for purchasing Treasury Bonds, allowing you to access these valuable assets for your investment needs. Let's proceed to Part 7: Purchasing Treasury Bonds.

PART 7: PURCHASING TREASURY BONDS

16: BUYING DIRECTLY FROM THE GOVERNMENT (TREASURYDIRECT)

Let's explore the process of buying Treasury Bonds directly from the government through TreasuryDirect—an online platform provided by the U.S. Department of the Treasury. TreasuryDirect offers individual investors a convenient and secure way to purchase and manage Treasury securities without the need for a broker or financial intermediary.

Setting Up a TreasuryDirect Account: To get started, you need to open a TreasuryDirect account on the official TreasuryDirect website (treasurydirect.gov). The account setup requires providing personal information, such as your Social Security number, mailing address, and bank account details for transactions.

Types of Treasury Securities Available: Through TreasuryDirect, you can purchase various Treasury securities, including Treasury Bills (T-Bills), Treasury Notes, Treasury Bonds, Treasury Inflation-Protected Securities (TIPS), and Savings Bonds.

Making Purchases: Once your account is set up, you can buy Treasury securities directly from the government through TreasuryDirect's BuyDirect feature. Select the type of security, the desired amount, and the purchase price or yield.

Auctions and Competitive Bidding: For some Treasury securities, such as T-Bills, Treasury Notes, and Treasury Bonds, you have the option to participate in auctions. In competitive bidding, you specify the yield you are willing to accept, and in non-competitive bidding, you agree to accept the yield determined by the auction results.

Direct Payroll Deduction and Tax Refunds: TreasuryDirect also offers the convenience of direct payroll deduction, allowing you to purchase Treasury securities automatically with a portion of your paycheck. Additionally, you can use your tax refund to buy Treasury securities through TreasuryDirect.

Holding and Managing Treasury Securities: All purchased Treasury securities are held electronically in your TreasuryDirect account. You can manage your holdings, reinvest interest, and view transaction history through the platform.

Interest Payments and Maturity: Interest payments for Treasury securities purchased through TreasuryDirect are deposited directly into your designated bank account. Upon maturity, the proceeds are also credited to your bank account.

Redemption and Selling: You can redeem or sell your Treasury securities before maturity, subject to market conditions and availability. TreasuryDirect provides options for early redemption or selling your securities to other investors in the secondary market.

Safety and Security: TreasuryDirect is a secure platform, and your holdings are protected by the U.S. government. The electronic format eliminates the risk of physical loss or theft of paper certificates.

Considerations and Limitations: While TreasuryDirect offers numerous advantages, it may not be suitable for everyone. Investors seeking more extensive investment options or guidance from a financial advisor may prefer using brokerage services.

Buying Treasury Bonds directly from the government through TreasuryDirect provides individual investors with a convenient and accessible way to access these low-risk securities. Whether you are purchasing Treasury Bills for short-term liquidity needs or investing in long-term Treasury Bonds for retirement planning, TreasuryDirect offers a user-friendly platform for managing your Treasury securities.

In the next chapter, we'll explore alternative methods of purchasing Treasury Bonds through brokerages and banks, providing a broader perspective on accessing these essential government securities. Let's proceed to Chapter 18: Purchasing through Brokerages and Banks.

17: PURCHASING TREASURY BONDS THROUGH BROKERAGES AND BANKS

In this chapter, we'll explore the process of purchasing Treasury Bonds through brokerages and banks. While buying directly from the government through TreasuryDirect is one option, many investors prefer using financial intermediaries to access Treasury Bonds and other investment opportunities.

BROKERAGE ACCOUNTS

A brokerage account is a type of investment account provided by brokerage firms that allows investors to buy and sell various securities, including Treasury Bonds. To get started, you need to open a brokerage account with a reputable brokerage firm.

TYPES OF BROKERAGES

There are two main types of brokerage firms: full-service and discount brokerages. Full-service brokerages offer personalized advice and a range of services, while discount brokerages provide a self-directed approach with lower fees.

ACCESS TO TREASURY BONDS

Most brokerage firms offer access to a wide range of Treasury Bonds, including Treasury Bills, Treasury Notes, and Treasury

Bonds with various maturities. You can search for available Treasury Bonds on the brokerage platform.

ONLINE TRADING

With online brokerage accounts, investors can place buy or sell orders for Treasury Bonds through a user-friendly online platform. You can specify the type of Treasury Bond, the desired amount, and the price or yield you are willing to accept.

COMMISSION AND FEES

Be aware of any commissions or fees associated with buying Treasury Bonds through a brokerage account. These costs can vary between full-service and discount brokerages, as well as between different brokerage firms.

BOND AUCTIONS

Some Treasury Bonds are sold through auctions, and brokerage firms can help you participate in these auctions. You can place competitive or non-competitive bids, depending on your preference for yield determination.

BANK OFFERINGS

In addition to brokerage accounts, you can also purchase Treasury Bonds through certain banks. Banks may offer direct sales of Treasury securities to their customers or provide access through brokerage services affiliated with the bank.

BOND LADDERS AND STRATEGIES

Brokerage firms and banks can assist investors in implementing bond laddering strategies, where they spread their Treasury Bond investments across different maturities to manage interest rate risk.

RESEARCH AND SUPPORT

Many brokerage firms offer research and educational resources to help investors make informed decisions about their Treasury Bond purchases. Additionally, customer support is available to address any questions or concerns.

ACCOUNT CONSOLIDATION

Investors with multiple investments and accounts may find it convenient to consolidate their Treasury Bond holdings with their other assets in a brokerage or bank account.

Using brokerages and banks to purchase Treasury Bonds can provide investors with a broad range of investment options, research tools, and support services. Whether you prefer a self-directed approach with a discount brokerage or personalized advice from a full-service firm, purchasing Treasury Bonds through these intermediaries offers flexibility and convenience.

In the next part of this guide, we'll explore essential considerations for holding and managing your Treasury Bond investments effectively. Let's proceed to Part 8: Holding Treasury Bonds.

PART 8: HOLDING TREASURY BONDS

18: MANAGING YOUR TREASURY BOND INVESTMENTS

Proactively managing your Treasury Bond investments is essential for optimizing returns and ensuring your portfolio remains aligned with your financial goals and risk tolerance. In this chapter, we'll explore essential considerations for managing your Treasury Bond investments effectively. Proper management ensures that your portfolio remains aligned with your financial goals, risk tolerance, and changing market conditions.

Regular Portfolio Review: Perform periodic reviews of your Treasury Bond portfolio to ensure it continues to meet your investment objectives. Assess your financial goals, risk tolerance, and time horizon to determine if any adjustments are necessary.

Rebalancing: Consider rebalancing your portfolio if the allocation of your Treasury Bonds deviates significantly from your target asset allocation. Rebalancing involves selling or buying assets to bring your portfolio back in line with your desired allocation.

Interest Payments and Reinvestment: Treasury Bonds pay periodic interest, and you have the option to reinvest these interest payments to compound your returns. You can reinvest the interest into new Treasury Bonds or other assets, depending on your investment strategy.

Maturity Considerations: As Treasury Bonds approach their maturity dates, evaluate your financial needs and market conditions to determine whether to reinvest in new bonds or reallocate the proceeds into other investments.

Interest Rate Environment: Keep an eye on changes in interest rates, as they can impact the value of your Treasury Bonds, particularly for longer-term bonds. In a rising interest rate environment, existing bond prices may decline, while falling interest rates can lead to capital appreciation.

Inflation Protection (TIPS): If you hold Treasury Inflation-Protected Securities (TIPS), monitor inflation rates and their potential impact on your investment. TIPS adjust their principal value with changes in the Consumer Price Index (CPI), providing a hedge against inflation.

Diversification and Risk Management: Review the diversification of your Treasury Bond holdings within your overall portfolio. Diversifying across different maturities and types of Treasury Bonds can help manage risk and provide stability.

Tax Considerations: Be aware of the tax implications of your Treasury Bond investments. Interest income from Treasury Bonds is subject to federal income tax, but it is exempt from state and local taxes.

Professional Advice: Consider seeking advice from a financial advisor, especially if you have a complex portfolio or are unsure about managing your Treasury Bond investments effectively.

Stay Informed: Stay informed about economic and market trends that may impact your Treasury Bond investments. Be aware of news and events that could affect interest rates and the overall bond market.

Regular reviews, rebalancing, and staying informed about market developments will help you make informed decisions and navigate changing market conditions. In the next chapter, we'll explore the option of reinvesting or cashing out your Treasury Bond investments and the considerations involved in each choice. Let's proceed to Chapter 20: Reinvesting or Cashing Out: Options and Considerations.

19: REINVESTING OR CASHING OUT

OPTIONS AND CONSIDERATIONS

As your Treasury Bonds approach maturity or if you need to access funds for other purposes, you have several options to consider. In this chapter, we'll explore the options of reinvesting or cashing out your Treasury Bond investments and the important considerations involved in each choice.

Reinvesting in New Treasury Bonds: If your Treasury Bonds are approaching maturity, you can choose to reinvest the proceeds into new Treasury Bonds. This option allows you to maintain exposure to Treasury securities and potentially continue earning interest on your investments.

Assessing Market Conditions: Before reinvesting, assess the prevailing market conditions and interest rate environment. Consider whether current interest rates are favorable for reinvestment or if waiting for potential rate increases might be more beneficial.

Diversification and Asset Allocation: Reinvesting provides an opportunity to reassess your asset allocation and diversification strategy. Consider how Treasury Bonds fit into your overall portfolio and whether adjustments are needed to align with your financial goals and risk tolerance.

Cashing Out: Cashing out your Treasury Bond investments involves selling them before maturity. This option can be useful if you need immediate access to funds for financial goals, emergencies, or other investments.

Secondary Market Sales: You can sell Treasury Bonds in the secondary market through brokerages or financial institutions. Keep in mind that the price you receive may be influenced by current interest rates and market demand.

Interest Rate Risk: Cashing out before maturity exposes you to interest rate risk. If you sell in a rising interest rate environment, you may receive a lower price for your bonds than their face value. Conversely, selling in a declining interest rate environment could result in capital gains.

Reinvestment Risk: Reinvesting in new Treasury Bonds also carries reinvestment risk. If you reinvest when interest rates are low, your new bonds may yield less than your original ones.

Tax Implications: Consider the tax implications of reinvesting or cashing out. Depending on your tax bracket and the timing of your transactions, you may have capital gains or losses to report for tax purposes.

Evaluating Financial Needs: Carefully assess your financial needs and goals before making a decision. If you have specific short-term or long-term financial requirements, cashing out or reinvesting may align with those needs.

Professional Advice: Seeking advice from a financial advisor can help you evaluate the best course of action based on your individual circumstances and investment objectives.

Ultimately, the decision to reinvest or cash out your Treasury Bond investments depends on your financial goals, risk tolerance, and market conditions. Both options have their advantages and considerations, and the choice should align with your broader investment strategy. Regularly review your investment plan and consult with a financial advisor to make well-informed decisions that support your financial well-being.

In the next part of this guide, we'll explore the relationship between interest rates and bond prices, providing insights into how changes in interest rates can impact your Treasury Bond investments. Let's proceed to Part 9: Understanding Interest Rates and Bond Prices.

PART 9: UNDERSTANDING INTEREST RATES AND BOND PRICES

20: RELATIONSHIP BETWEEN INTEREST RATES AND BOND PRICES

Understanding how changes in interest rates affect bond prices is essential for making informed decisions in managing your bond portfolio. In this chapter, we'll delve deeper into the fundamental relationship between interest rates and bond prices, a critical concept to grasp for investors in Treasury Bonds and other fixed-income securities.

BOND PRICE SENSITIVITY TO INTEREST RATES

The price of a bond is inversely related to changes in interest rates. When interest rates rise, the prices of existing bonds generally fall, and when interest rates decline, bond prices tend to rise. This inverse relationship is crucial to comprehend when analyzing the impact of interest rate movements on your bond investments.

COUPON RATE VS. YIELD

A bond's coupon rate represents the fixed interest rate the bond pays based on its face value. However, the yield of a bond is determined by its current market price and represents the effective interest rate an investor earns on the bond. If a bond's yield is higher than its coupon rate, its price will be below its face value, and vice versa.

BOND PRICE AND YIELD CHANGES

As interest rates rise, newly issued bonds will offer higher yields to attract investors. Consequently, existing bonds with lower yields become less attractive, leading to a decline in their market value. Conversely, when interest rates fall, existing bonds with higher yields become more appealing, causing their market value to rise.

MATURITY AND PRICE SENSITIVITY

Longer-term bonds are generally more sensitive to interest rate changes than shorter-term bonds. This means that long-term Treasury Bonds will experience more significant price fluctuations in response to interest rate movements compared to short-term Treasury Bills.

INTEREST RATE RISK

Interest rate risk is the potential for bond prices to fluctuate due to changes in interest rates. Investors who sell their bonds before maturity may be exposed to this risk, as they may receive a price below the bond's face value if interest rates have risen since the bond's issuance.

HOLDING BONDS TO MATURITY

If you hold Treasury Bonds until they mature, you will receive the full face value of the bond, regardless of interest rate fluctuations. This makes holding bonds to maturity a way to mitigate interest rate risk.

REINVESTMENT RISK

Reinvestment risk refers to the risk that when your bonds mature and you reinvest the proceeds, you may have to reinvest at lower interest rates than when you initially purchased the bonds.

MARKET SENTIMENT AND BOND PRICES

Market sentiment can also influence bond prices. In times of economic uncertainty, investors may flock to the safety of bonds, driving up bond prices and pushing yields lower.

ECONOMIC FACTORS AND INTEREST RATES

Various economic factors, such as inflation, economic growth, and central bank policies, influence interest rates. Understanding these factors can provide insights into potential changes in interest rates and bond prices.

MANAGING INTEREST RATE RISK

Investors can manage interest rate risk by diversifying their bond holdings, considering shorter-term bonds, and employing bond laddering strategies to stagger maturities.

Being aware of the relationship between interest rates and bond prices empowers investors to make informed decisions in managing their bond portfolios. Whether you aim to capitalize on favorable interest rate movements or hedge against interest rate risk, understanding this dynamic will help you optimize your investment strategy.

In the next chapter, we'll explore strategies for low-risk investing using Treasury Bonds, offering various approaches suitable for different investment objectives. Let's proceed to Chapter 21: Impact of Economic Factors on Treasury Bond Market.

21: IMPACT OF ECONOMIC FACTORS ON TREASURY BOND MARKET

As fixed-income securities, Treasury Bonds are sensitive to various economic conditions and indicators. Understanding these factors can provide insights into how the bond market behaves and help investors make informed decisions about their Treasury Bond investments.

INFLATION

Inflation, the rate at which the general level of prices for goods and services rises, has a substantial impact on Treasury Bond prices. When inflation is high or expected to rise, bond investors may demand higher yields to compensate for the eroding purchasing power of their future interest payments. As a result, bond prices may fall when inflation expectations increase.

INTEREST RATES AND MONETARY POLICY

Central banks, like the Federal Reserve in the United States, influence short-term interest rates through monetary policy. Changes in these rates can ripple through the bond market. For example, when the central bank raises its benchmark interest rate to combat inflation, it may lead to higher yields in the bond market, pushing bond prices down.

ECONOMIC GROWTH AND EMPLOYMENT

Economic indicators such as Gross Domestic Product (GDP) growth and employment data can impact the bond market. Strong economic growth and low unemployment may lead to expectations of higher inflation and interest rates, causing bond prices to decline.

FEDERAL RESERVE ACTIONS

The actions and statements of the Federal Reserve, particularly regarding monetary policy and interest rate decisions, can significantly influence the bond market. Investors closely monitor Federal Reserve meetings and announcements for hints about future policy directions.

MARKET SENTIMENT AND RISK APPETITE

Market sentiment and risk appetite can drive investors' behavior in the bond market. During periods of economic uncertainty or geopolitical tensions, investors may seek the safety of Treasury Bonds, driving up bond prices and pushing yields lower.

CURRENCY AND EXCHANGE RATES

Fluctuations in currency values and exchange rates can impact the demand for Treasury Bonds by foreign investors. Changes in exchange rates may influence the attractiveness of Treasury Bonds denominated in a specific currency.

GLOBAL ECONOMIC CONDITIONS

The global economic environment can affect Treasury Bond yields and prices. Economic developments in major economies worldwide may impact investors' perceptions of the U.S. economy and the attractiveness of Treasury Bonds relative to other assets.

SUPPLY AND DEMAND DYNAMICS

Changes in the supply and demand for Treasury Bonds can influence their prices. Increased demand from investors or reduced bond issuance by the government may lead to higher bond prices.

FISCAL POLICY AND GOVERNMENT BUDGETS

Fiscal policies, such as tax cuts or increased government spending, can impact economic growth and inflation expectations, affecting bond yields and prices.

INFLATION-PROTECTED SECURITIES (TIPS) PERFORMANCE

The performance of Treasury Inflation-Protected Securities (TIPS) can provide insights into investors' inflation expectations, which can, in turn, influence nominal Treasury Bond prices.

Being mindful of the economic factors that influence the Treasury Bond market empowers investors to make informed decisions. Monitoring these factors can help you understand the potential drivers behind bond price movements and better position your Treasury Bond investments in line with your financial objectives and risk tolerance.

In the next chapter, we'll explore various low-risk investing strategies using Treasury Bonds, providing insights into different approaches to suit your investment goals. Let's proceed to Let's proceed to Part 10: Strategies for Low-Risk Investing

PART 10: STRATEGIES FOR LOW-RISK INVESTING

22: BUY-AND-HOLD STRATEGY

The buy-and-hold strategy is a long-term investment approach that involves purchasing securities, including Treasury Bonds, and holding them for an extended period, often years or even decades. This strategy is rooted in the belief that, over time, well-managed assets tend to appreciate in value and provide a reliable source of income.

Stability and Low-Risk Focus: The buy-and-hold strategy is particularly well-suited for investors seeking stability and lower risk in their portfolio. Treasury Bonds, being considered one of the safest investments, align well with this approach.

Capital Preservation: By holding onto Treasury Bonds until maturity, investors can preserve their capital and be assured of receiving the bond's face value, as Treasury Bonds are backed by the full faith and credit of the U.S. government.

Consistent Income Stream: Treasury Bonds pay periodic interest, providing investors with a steady income stream. This predictable cash flow can be beneficial, especially for retirees or those relying on investment income.

Potential for Price Appreciation: While the primary goal of the buy-and-hold strategy is capital preservation, there is also potential for price appreciation over time, especially if interest rates decline after the bonds are purchased.

Mitigating Short-Term Volatility: By adopting a long-term perspective, investors can avoid making impulsive decisions in response to short-term market fluctuations. This can reduce emotional reactions and keep investors focused on their long-term goals.

Reinvestment Opportunities: As interest payments are received on Treasury Bonds, investors can reinvest those funds into new bonds or other assets, compounding their returns over time.

Monitoring and Periodic Review: Although the buy-and-hold strategy advocates maintaining a long-term perspective, it does not imply a complete disregard for portfolio monitoring. Periodic reviews are essential to ensure that the portfolio remains aligned with changing financial goals and risk tolerance.

Tax Efficiency: Holding Treasury Bonds until maturity can also offer tax efficiency, as investors can defer reporting interest income until the bonds mature or are sold.

Tailoring Your Portfolio: The buy-and-hold strategy can be applied in various ways, depending on individual investment goals and risk tolerance. Investors can tailor their portfolios by selecting different types of Treasury Bonds with varying maturities and coupon rates to suit their needs.

Diversification: While the buy-and-hold strategy is focused on long-term holdings, it does not dismiss the importance of diversification. Investors may choose to diversify their bond portfolio by including other low-risk assets to spread risk effectively.

The buy-and-hold strategy is not without its potential drawbacks. Market conditions and economic factors can change over time, affecting the performance of investments. Moreover, this strategy requires discipline and patience, as it may take years to realize significant capital appreciation.

The buy-and-hold strategy with Treasury Bonds can be an effective approach for investors seeking stability, income, and long-term capital preservation. By maintaining a disciplined, long-term perspective and periodically reviewing their portfolio, investors can leverage the benefits of Treasury Bonds while staying on track to achieve their financial goals.

In the next chapter, we'll explore another low-risk investing strategy known as "laddering," which involves staggering maturities to manage interest rate risk. Let's proceed to Chapter 23: Laddering Your Treasury Bonds.

23: LADDERING YOUR TREASURY BONDS

L addering is an investment strategy that involves dividing your Treasury Bond portfolio into multiple bonds with staggered maturities. This approach aims to spread risk, maintain liquidity, and potentially capture the benefits of both short-term and long-term bonds. In this chapter, we'll explore the concept of laddering and how it can be applied to Treasury Bonds.

Understanding Laddering: Laddering is like building a "staircase" of bonds with different maturity dates. Each "rung" represents a bond with a specific maturity, such as one, three, five, or ten years. As each bond matures, the proceeds can be reinvested in new bonds at the longest end of the ladder.

Spreading Risk: By diversifying maturities, laddering helps mitigate interest rate risk. Short-term bonds are less sensitive to interest rate changes, providing stability in times of rising rates. Meanwhile, long-term bonds offer the potential for higher yields and may benefit from falling interest rates.

Maintaining Liquidity: With a ladder, you have bonds maturing at regular intervals. This provides a consistent source of liquidity, allowing you to access funds periodically without having to sell all your bonds at once.

Reducing Reinvestment Risk: Laddering helps address reinvestment risk—the concern that when your bonds mature, you'll have to reinvest at lower interest rates. By reinvesting regularly, you can take advantage of higher yields when interest rates rise.

Customizing Your Ladder: You can tailor your ladder to match your financial goals and risk tolerance. For instance, you might choose a short-term ladder if you need frequent access to funds, or a longer-term ladder for potential higher yields.

Assessing Market Conditions: When constructing or managing your ladder, consider current market conditions and interest rate trends. This will help you determine the optimal mix of short-term and long-term bonds.

Laddering with TIPS: Laddering can be applied to Treasury Inflation-Protected Securities (TIPS) as well. By holding a ladder of TIPS, you can hedge against inflation while managing interest rate risk.

Periodic Rebalancing: Regularly rebalancing your ladder involves reinvesting the proceeds from maturing bonds into new ones at the longest end of the ladder. This helps maintain the ladder's structure and alignment with your investment goals.

Long-Term Planning: Laddering is a long-term strategy, allowing you to plan for future financial needs and goals. Whether it's funding education expenses, retirement, or major purchases, the ladder provides a disciplined approach to achieve these objectives.

Professional Guidance: If you're new to laddering or unsure how to implement it effectively, consider seeking advice from a financial advisor. They can help you design a ladder that suits your unique financial situation and objectives.

Laddering Treasury Bonds can be a prudent and flexible strategy, offering a balance between stability and potential returns. By spreading your investments across different maturities, you can enhance your ability to weather changing interest rate environments while positioning yourself for long-term financial success.

In the next chapter, we'll explore how Treasury Bonds can be utilized as a hedge in your investment portfolio. Let's proceed to Chapter 24: Using Treasury Bonds as a Hedge.

24: USING TREASURY BONDS AS A HEDGE

In this chapter, we'll explore how Treasury Bonds can be utilized as a hedge in your investment portfolio. A hedge is an investment strategy designed to offset potential losses in one asset by holding another asset with a negative correlation to the first. Treasury Bonds, known for their low-risk nature and inverse relationship with equities, can serve as an effective hedge in certain market conditions.

Safe-Haven Asset: During periods of market volatility, economic uncertainty, or geopolitical tensions, investors often seek safe-haven assets to protect their portfolios. Treasury Bonds, backed by the U.S. government, are considered one of the safest investments and tend to perform well when other riskier assets experience turmoil.

Inverse Correlation with Equities: Treasury Bonds have historically exhibited an inverse correlation with equities. When stock prices decline, investors often seek refuge in Treasury Bonds, driving up their prices and lowering their yields. This negative correlation can help balance your portfolio and reduce overall risk.

Diversification Benefits: Adding Treasury Bonds to a diversified investment portfolio can enhance its risk-adjusted returns. The low correlation between Treasury Bonds and other assets can lead to better portfolio performance during challenging market conditions.

Managing Interest Rate Risk: Treasury Bonds can also act as a hedge against interest rate risk. When interest rates rise, bond prices tend to fall. By holding Treasury Bonds, you can potentially offset losses in other fixed-income investments due to rising rates.

Hedging Against Inflation: For investors concerned about the impact of inflation on their portfolio, Treasury Inflation-Protected Securities (TIPS) can act as an inflation hedge. TIPS adjust their principal value based on changes in the Consumer Price Index (CPI), protecting investors from inflationary pressures.

Tailoring Your Hedge: The extent to which Treasury Bonds serve as a hedge depends on your risk tolerance and investment objectives. You can adjust the allocation of Treasury Bonds in your portfolio to tailor the hedge according to your specific needs.

Rebalancing and Monitoring: To maintain an effective hedge, it's essential to regularly rebalance your portfolio and monitor market conditions. Adjusting your allocation of Treasury Bonds based on changing economic or market trends can optimize the effectiveness of the hedge.

Complementing Other Hedges: In addition to Treasury Bonds, you may use other hedging strategies, such as options or inverse ETFs, to further protect your portfolio from specific risks or market downturns. Combining multiple hedges can create a well-rounded risk management approach.

Considerations for Different Investors: While Treasury Bonds can be a suitable hedge for many investors, their role as a hedge may vary depending on individual circumstances. Factors such as investment goals, time horizon, and risk tolerance should be considered when incorporating Treasury Bonds into your hedge.

Professional Guidance: Utilizing Treasury Bonds as a hedge can be complex, especially when considering the nuances of different Treasury securities and their impact on a diversified portfolio. Seeking guidance from a financial advisor can help you design a hedge that aligns with your specific investment needs and objectives.

Using Treasury Bonds as a hedge can be an effective risk management strategy for investors seeking to protect their portfolios from market volatility and economic uncertainties. By understanding the inverse correlation between Treasury Bonds and equities, you can leverage these bonds to add stability and potential protection to your investment holdings.

In the next part of this guide, we'll explore different low-risk investing strategies that can be employed using Treasury Bonds. Let's proceed to Part 10: Strategies for Low-Risk Investing.

PART 11: MONITORING AND MANAGING YOUR PORTFOLIO

25: TRACKING PERFORMANCE AND YIELD

In this chapter, we'll explore how to track the performance and yield of your Treasury Bond investments. Monitoring these factors is essential for assessing the health of your portfolio and making informed decisions about your bond holdings.

Total Return Calculation: To track the performance of your Treasury Bonds, you need to calculate the total return. The total return considers both the interest income (coupon payments) and any capital appreciation or depreciation of the bonds. It provides a comprehensive view of how your investments are performing.

Yield to Maturity (YTM): The yield to maturity (YTM) is a crucial metric for assessing the potential return on your Treasury Bonds if you hold them until maturity. YTM considers the bond's current price, its coupon rate, and the time left to maturity. It helps you compare the potential returns of different bonds.

Current Yield: Current yield is another important metric to track, especially for investors who hold Treasury Bonds outside of maturity. It measures the bond's annual interest income as a percentage of its current market price. Unlike YTM, current yield doesn't consider capital gains or losses.

Tracking Interest Payments: Keep a record of the interest payments you receive from your Treasury Bonds. This information is crucial for budgeting and assessing the income generated by your bond investments.

Price Movements: Track the prices of your Treasury Bonds over time. Price movements can indicate how changes in interest rates and market conditions affect the value of your bond holdings.

Comparing Against Benchmarks: Compare the performance of your Treasury Bond investments against relevant benchmarks, such as the broader bond market or specific Treasury Bond indices. This comparison will provide insights into how your portfolio performs relative to the broader market.

Evaluating Performance Against Goals: Regularly evaluate the performance of your Treasury Bonds against your financial goals and risk tolerance. Ensure that your bond investments align with your objectives and that they continue to meet your expectations.

Rebalancing When Needed: Based on your portfolio performance and changes in your financial goals, consider rebalancing your Treasury Bond holdings. Rebalancing involves adjusting your asset allocation to maintain your desired risk level and returns.

Keeping Up with Economic Indicators: Stay informed about economic indicators and trends that could impact interest rates and the bond market. Economic factors play a significant role in determining bond yields and prices.

Utilizing Technology and Tools: Take advantage of various financial tools and technology that can help you track the performance and yield of your Treasury Bond investments. Many brokerage platforms and investment apps provide features to monitor your portfolio effectively.

By consistently tracking the performance and yield of your Treasury Bond investments, you can make well-informed decisions about your portfolio and adjust your strategy as needed. Whether you're aiming for steady income, capital preservation, or diversification, keeping a close eye on these metrics will support your overall financial objectives.

In the next chapter, we'll explore how to rebalance your Treasury Bond portfolio to maintain your desired asset allocation. Let's proceed to Chapter 26: Rebalancing Your Treasury Bond Portfolio.

26: REBALANCING YOUR TREASURY BOND PORTFOLIO

R ebalancing is a crucial aspect of maintaining your desired asset allocation and risk level over time. As the market fluctuates and your financial goals evolve, rebalancing ensures that your bond holdings remain aligned with your investment strategy. In this chapter, we'll delve into the process of rebalancing your Treasury Bond portfolio.

Understanding Rebalancing: Rebalancing involves adjusting the allocation of your Treasury Bond holdings to bring them back in line with your target asset allocation. Over time, market movements may cause the proportion of bonds in your portfolio to drift from your intended allocation.

Setting Rebalancing Thresholds: Establish specific thresholds or triggers for when you should rebalance your portfolio. For instance, you might decide to rebalance if the allocation to Treasury Bonds deviates by more than a certain percentage from your target allocation.

Rebalancing Frequency: The frequency of rebalancing depends on your investment strategy and preferences. Some investors choose to rebalance on a regular schedule, such as annually or semi-annually, while others rebalance based on specific events or market conditions.

Consider Transaction Costs and Taxes: When rebalancing, be mindful of transaction costs, such as brokerage fees, which can impact your returns. Additionally, consider the tax implications of selling bonds, especially if you hold them in taxable accounts.

Assessing Financial Goals: Before rebalancing, reassess your financial goals, risk tolerance, and time horizon. Changes in your circumstances may necessitate adjustments to your asset allocation.

Cash Flow Needs: Take into account any cash flow needs you may have, such as upcoming expenses or investment contributions. Rebalancing can be an opportunity to align your bond holdings with these requirements.

Evaluating Economic Conditions: Keep an eye on economic indicators and market trends that may impact interest rates and bond prices. Economic conditions can influence the performance of your Treasury Bond portfolio.

Consider Your Entire Portfolio: Rebalancing shouldn't be limited to Treasury Bonds alone. Consider your entire investment portfolio and how different asset classes interact. Rebalancing across all your holdings can ensure a well-diversified and balanced approach.

Gradual Rebalancing: You don't need to make significant changes all at once. Gradual rebalancing allows you to adjust your portfolio over time, reducing the potential impact of sudden market movements.

Seek Professional Advice: If you're uncertain about rebalancing or if your financial situation is complex, consider seeking guidance from a financial advisor. An advisor can help you determine the most suitable rebalancing approach based on your individual circumstances.

Rebalancing your Treasury Bond portfolio is a proactive strategy to maintain the desired risk and return profile of your invest-ments. By periodically reassessing your asset allocation, making thoughtful adjustments, and staying aligned with your financial goals, you can optimize the performance and effectiveness of your bond holdings.

In the next part of this guide, we'll explore the tax considerations related to investing in Treasury Bonds. Understanding the tax im-plications can help you make more informed decisions and maxi-mize the after-tax returns of your bond investments. Let's proceed to Part 12: Tax Considerations.

PART 12: TAX CONSIDERATIONS

27: TAXATION OF TREASURY BOND INTEREST

Understanding the tax implications is essential for effectively managing your bond investments and maximizing your after-tax returns. In this chapter, we'll explore the taxation of Treasury Bond interest and how it can impact your investment returns.

Taxable Interest Income: The interest income you receive from Treasury Bonds is generally considered taxable at the federal level. This means the interest you earn is subject to federal income tax.

Federal Tax Treatment: The interest income from Treasury Bonds is taxed at your ordinary income tax rate. The rate you pay depends on your tax bracket, which is determined by your total income and filing status.

State and Local Taxes: In addition to federal taxes, the interest income from Treasury Bonds may also be subject to state and local income taxes, depending on the tax laws in your state of residence. Some states do not levy income taxes, providing a tax advantage for residents in those locations.

Tax-Advantaged Accounts: Investing in Treasury Bonds through tax-advantaged accounts, such as Individual Retirement Accounts (IRAs) or 401(k) plans, can provide tax benefits. In these accounts, your interest income may grow tax-deferred or even tax-free, depending on the type of account.

Tax-Exempt Treasury Bonds: Certain Treasury Bonds, such as Treasury Bonds issued by U.S. territories or possessions, may be tax-exempt at the federal level. These bonds can provide income that is free from federal income taxes, making them attractive to investors in higher tax brackets.

Reporting Interest Income: At the end of each tax year, you will receive a Form 1099-INT from the institution that holds your Treasury Bonds. This form reports the total interest income you earned during the year and should be used when filing your income tax return.

Tax Efficiency Considerations: When constructing your investment portfolio, consider the tax efficiency of your holdings. For example, holding Treasury Bonds in tax-advantaged accounts can help reduce the immediate tax burden on the interest income.

Muni Bonds vs. Treasury Bonds: Comparing the tax implications of Treasury Bonds with municipal bonds (muni bonds) is essential. Muni bonds are often exempt from federal income taxes and, in some cases, state and local taxes, making them an attractive option for investors seeking tax-free income.

Tax-Loss Harvesting: In certain situations, you may incur losses on other investments in your portfolio. Utilizing tax-loss harvesting strategies can help offset taxable gains from Treasury Bond interest income.

Consult a Tax Professional: The tax implications of investing in Treasury Bonds can be complex, especially when considering your specific financial situation and tax laws. Consulting with a qualified tax professional can provide personalized advice and help you optimize your tax strategy.

Being aware of the tax treatment of Treasury Bond interest is essential for budgeting and planning your overall investment strategy. By understanding the tax implications and exploring tax-efficient investment options, you can make more informed decisions and maximize the after-tax returns of your Treasury Bond investments.

In the next chapter, we'll explore additional tax efficiency strategies and considerations for optimizing the tax benefits of your bond holdings. Let's proceed to Chapter 28: Strategies for Tax Efficiency.

28: STRATEGIES FOR TAX EFFICIENCY

By managing your bonds in a tax-efficient manner, you can potentially reduce your tax liability and enhance your after-tax returns. In this chapter, we'll explore various strategies for optimizing the tax efficiency of your Treasury Bond investments.

Tax-Advantaged Accounts: Utilize tax-advantaged accounts, such as Individual Retirement Accounts (IRAs) or 401(k) plans, to hold your Treasury Bonds. These accounts offer tax benefits, such as tax-deferred or tax-free growth, depending on the type of account. By sheltering your bond investments in these accounts, you can defer taxes on the interest income until you make withdrawals during retirement.

Tax-Exempt Treasury Bonds: Consider investing in tax-exempt Treasury Bonds, such as those issued by U.S. territories or possessions. The interest income from these bonds is generally exempt from federal income tax, making them attractive for investors in higher tax brackets.

Asset Location Strategy: Implement an asset location strategy, where you strategically allocate your investments across different types of accounts to maximize tax efficiency. For example, consider holding tax-efficient investments, like Treasury Bonds, in taxable brokerage accounts, while keeping tax-inefficient assets in tax-advantaged accounts.

Hold-to-Maturity Strategy: Holding Treasury Bonds until maturity can provide tax benefits, as you'll only pay taxes on the interest income when the bonds mature or are sold. This approach minimizes the impact of annual taxable events that may occur with more frequent trading.

Tax-Loss Harvesting: Use tax-loss harvesting to offset gains from other investments with losses in your portfolio. Selling certain assets at a loss can help reduce your overall taxable income, potentially lowering your tax liability on Treasury Bond interest income.

Municipal Bonds (Muni Bonds): Consider adding municipal bonds (muni bonds) to your portfolio. Muni bonds are typically exempt from federal income tax, and in some cases, state and local taxes as well. Including these tax-free bonds can enhance your tax efficiency and provide a source of tax-free income.

Hold Long-Term for Lower Capital Gains Tax: If you plan to sell your Treasury Bonds before maturity, consider holding them for more than one year to qualify for the long-term capital gains tax rate, which is typically lower than the ordinary income tax rate.

Tax-Efficient Rebalancing: When rebalancing your portfolio, be mindful of potential tax implications. Focus on adjusting your asset allocation without triggering unnecessary taxable events.

Consider ETFs or Mutual Funds: Investing in Treasury Bond exchange-traded funds (ETFs) or mutual funds can offer tax efficiency benefits, as they may have lower turnover and capital gains distributions compared to individual bonds.

Professional Tax Advice: Navigating the intricacies of tax efficiency can be challenging. Seeking advice from a tax professional or financial advisor with expertise in tax planning can help you develop a personalized strategy that aligns with your financial goals.

Implementing tax-efficient strategies with your Treasury Bond investments can make a significant difference in your after-tax returns. By taking advantage of tax-advantaged accounts, tax-exempt bonds, and other tax-efficient investment approaches, you can optimize the tax benefits of your bond portfolio.

In the next part of this guide, we'll explore common pitfalls and mistakes to avoid when investing in Treasury Bonds, as well as tips for maximizing your returns while minimizing risks. Let's proceed to Part 13: Tips for Success and Common Pitfalls.

PART 13: TIPS FOR SUCCESS AND COMMON PITFALLS

29: AVOIDING COMMON MISTAKES

In this chapter, we'll discuss some common mistakes that investors often make when investing in Treasury Bonds and how to avoid them. Being aware of these pitfalls can help you make more informed decisions and enhance the success of your bond investments.

1. Ignoring Your Investment Objectives: One of the most significant mistakes is investing in Treasury Bonds without a clear understanding of your financial goals and risk tolerance. Always align your bond investments with your objectives to ensure they serve their intended purpose in your portfolio.

2. Chasing Yield: Avoid solely focusing on the highest yielding Treasury Bonds without considering the associated risks. Higher yields often come with increased risk, so it's crucial to strike a balance between yield and risk that matches your investment strategy.

3. Overlooking Diversification: Failing to diversify your Treasury Bond holdings can expose your portfolio to unnecessary risk. Diversification across various maturities and types of Treasury Bonds can help mitigate risk and improve overall stability.

4. Market Timing Mistakes: Attempting to time the market and predict interest rate movements can be challenging and risky. Avoid making sudden changes to your bond portfolio based on short-term market fluctuations, as this may lead to suboptimal results.

5. Neglecting Rebalancing: Neglecting to rebalance your Treasury Bond portfolio can result in unintended asset allocation drift. Regularly rebalancing can help maintain your desired risk level and alignment with your financial goals.

6. Holding Too Much in Cash: While holding some cash for emergencies is prudent, keeping excessive amounts in cash can lead to missed opportunities for potential returns from Treasury Bonds. Find the right balance between liquidity and investment.

7. Failing to Monitor Economic Indicators: Market conditions and economic factors can impact Treasury Bond performance. Stay informed about economic indicators and trends that may influence interest rates and bond prices.

8. Ignoring Tax Considerations: Taxes can significantly impact your bond returns. Ignoring tax considerations, such as investing in tax-advantaged accounts or tax-free municipal bonds, can result in missed opportunities for tax efficiency.

9. Not Seeking Professional Advice: Investing in Treasury Bonds can be complex, especially when considering your unique financial situation. Consulting with a financial advisor or tax professional can provide valuable guidance tailored to your needs.

10. Panic Selling During Market Volatility: Reacting impulsively to market volatility and panic selling can lead to suboptimal outcomes. Stay focused on your long-term investment strategy and avoid making decisions based on emotions.

By avoiding these common mistakes and adopting a disciplined approach to investing in Treasury Bonds, you can enhance the effectiveness of your bond portfolio and work toward achieving your financial goals.

In the next chapter, we'll provide valuable tips for maximizing your returns while minimizing risks when investing in Treasury Bonds. Let's proceed to Chapter 30: Tips for Maximizing Returns while Minimizing Risks.

30: TIPS FOR MAXIMIZING RETURNS WHILE MINIMIZING RISKS

I n this chapter, we'll explore valuable tips for optimizing the returns of your Treasury Bond investments while managing risks effectively. By employing these strategies, you can enhance the overall performance of your bond portfolio.

Maintain a Long-Term Perspective: Treasury Bonds are typically considered long-term investments. Holding them until maturity can help you capture their full potential returns and reduce the impact of short-term market fluctuations.

Align with Your Financial Goals: Ensure that your Treasury Bond investments align with your financial goals, time horizon, and risk tolerance. A well-matched bond portfolio can provide stability and support your long-term objectives.

Diversify Across Maturities: Spread your investments across different maturities, such as short-term, medium-term, and long-term Treasury Bonds. Diversification can help balance risk and provide potential opportunities for yield enhancement.

Consider Inflation Protection: Including Treasury Inflation-Protected Securities (TIPS) in your bond portfolio can safeguard against inflation risk. TIPS adjust their principal value with changes in inflation, providing a hedge against rising prices.

Rebalance Regularly: Regularly rebalancing your Treasury Bond portfolio helps maintain your desired asset allocation and risk exposure. This disciplined approach ensures that your portfolio stays aligned with your investment strategy.

Use Laddering to Manage Interest Rates: Laddering your Treasury Bonds allows you to manage interest rate risk effectively. By holding bonds with staggered maturities, you can take advantage of rising interest rates and maintain liquidity.

Consider Tax Efficiency: Utilize tax-efficient strategies, such as investing in tax-advantaged accounts or tax-exempt Treasury Bonds, to enhance your after-tax returns and minimize the impact of taxes on your bond income.

Avoid Chasing Yield: Be cautious of chasing high yields without considering the associated risks. Seek a balanced approach that matches your risk tolerance and investment objectives.

Stay Informed About Economic Conditions: Keep abreast of economic indicators and market trends that may influence interest rates and bond performance. Staying informed helps you make well-informed decisions.

Avoid Market Timing: Resist the temptation to time the market or make abrupt changes to your bond holdings based on short-term market movements. Stick to your long-term investment plan.

Seek Professional Advice: If you're unsure about the best approach for your Treasury Bond investments or have complex financial needs, consider seeking advice from a qualified financial advisor. A professional can provide personalized guidance to optimize your bond portfolio.

Periodically Review and Adjust: Regularly review your bond portfolio to ensure it aligns with your changing financial goals and risk tolerance. Adjust your holdings as needed to remain on track with your investment plan.

By following these tips, you can create a well-structured and disciplined Treasury Bond portfolio that maximizes potential returns while minimizing risks. Remember that investing in bonds involves careful consideration, and it's essential to tailor your approach to your unique financial circumstances and goals.

In the next part of this guide, we'll explore other low-risk investments that can complement Treasury Bonds in a well-diversified portfolio. Let's proceed to Part 14: Beyond Treasury Bonds: Exploring Other Low-Risk Investments.

PART 14: BEYOND TREASURY BONDS

EXPLORING OTHER LOW-RISK INVESTMENTS

31: CERTIFICATES OF DEPOSIT (CDS)

C Ds are a popular choice for investors seeking stability and predictable returns, making them an essential component of a diversified portfolio. In this chapter, we'll explore Certificates of Deposit (CDs) as a low-risk investment option and how they compare to Treasury Bonds.

Understanding Certificates of Deposit (CDs): Certificates of Deposit (CDs) are time deposits offered by banks and credit unions. They are considered low-risk investments because they are backed by the issuing financial institution and insured by the Federal Deposit Insurance Corporation (FDIC) in the United States, providing protection for up to a certain amount per account holder per institution.

Fixed Terms and Maturity: CDs have fixed terms, typically ranging from a few months to several years. During this period, you agree not to withdraw the funds, and in return, the financial institution pays you a fixed interest rate. At the end of the term (maturity), you receive the original principal plus the accrued interest.

Predictable Returns: The fixed interest rate of CDs offers predictability, ensuring that you know exactly how much you'll earn over the term. This can be advantageous for investors who prioritize stable and guaranteed returns.

Comparing CDs to Treasury Bonds: Both CDs and Treasury Bonds are considered low-risk investments, but there are some key differences. Treasury Bonds are issued by the U.S. government and have maturities that can extend up to 30 years. They are considered one of the safest investments globally. On the other hand, CDs are issued by banks or credit unions, have shorter maturities, and offer slightly higher interest rates than Treasury Bonds with similar maturities.

Liquidity Considerations: Unlike Treasury Bonds, which can be sold on the secondary market, CDs generally have limited liquidity until their maturity. Withdrawing funds from a CD before its maturity may result in a penalty, reducing the interest earned.

FDIC Insurance: The FDIC insures CDs up to $250,000 per account holder per institution. This insurance coverage protects your principal and interest from loss due to bank failure, making CDs a safe option for preserving capital.

CD Laddering Strategy: Similar to laddering with Treasury Bonds, investors can implement a CD laddering strategy to diversify maturities and ensure a steady stream of income. By purchasing CDs with different terms, you can have regular access to funds while benefiting from higher interest rates on longer-term CDs.

Early Withdrawal Penalties: It's essential to be aware of any early withdrawal penalties associated with CDs. These penalties are typically a certain number of months' worth of interest and can vary based on the term of the CD.

Reinvestment Risk: When a CD matures, you face reinvestment risk, which is the risk of having to reinvest your funds at a lower interest rate if prevailing rates have decreased.

Evaluating Your Investment Objectives: Consider your investment objectives, time horizon, and liquidity needs when deciding between Treasury Bonds and CDs. While both offer low-risk characteristics, CDs may be more suitable for shorter-term goals or when you prioritize capital preservation and predictable returns.

Certificates of Deposit (CDs) can be an attractive option for risk-averse investors seeking safety and predictability in their investments. By understanding the features of CDs and their role within a well-diversified portfolio, you can make informed decisions to meet your financial objectives.

In the next chapter, we'll explore another low-risk investment option: Money Market Funds. Let's proceed to Chapter 32: Money Market Funds.

32: MONEY MARKET FUNDS

Money Market Funds are popular choices for investors seeking stability, liquidity, and modest returns on their cash holdings. In this chapter, we'll explore Money Market Funds as a low-risk investment option and how they differ from Treasury Bonds and Certificates of Deposit (CDs).

Understanding Money Market Funds: Money Market Funds are mutual funds that invest in short-term, low-risk securities, such as Treasury Bills, certificates of deposit, commercial paper, and other highly liquid instruments. These funds aim to maintain a stable Net Asset Value (NAV) of $1 per share, making them a stable investment option.

Low Risk and High Liquidity: Money Market Funds are considered low-risk investments due to their focus on short-term, high-quality securities. They offer high liquidity, allowing investors to quickly access their funds without incurring penalties.

Stability of Principal: The primary objective of Money Market Funds is to preserve the principal investment while providing a return comparable to short-term interest rates.

Diversification: Money Market Funds invest in a diversified portfolio of money market instruments, spreading risk across various issuers and securities.

Comparing Money Market Funds to Treasury Bonds and CDs: While Money Market Funds share some characteristics with

Treasury Bonds and CDs, there are significant differences. Treasury Bonds have longer maturities and provide higher yields compared to Money Market Funds. CDs have fixed terms and offer slightly higher interest rates than Money Market Funds with similar maturities. Unlike Money Market Funds, CDs may have penalties for early withdrawals.

Yield and Returns: Money Market Fund returns are influenced by short-term interest rates set by the central bank. As interest rates change, the yield of these funds may fluctuate.

Money Market Funds vs. Savings Accounts: Money Market Funds are often compared to traditional savings accounts offered by banks. While both offer stability and liquidity, Money Market Funds may provide slightly higher yields and are managed by investment companies.

Money Market Fund Expenses: Money Market Funds charge expenses known as the expense ratio. This fee covers the fund's operating costs and is expressed as a percentage of the fund's assets.

Evaluating Investment Objectives: Consider your investment objectives and time horizon when choosing between Money Market Funds, Treasury Bonds, and CDs. If you prioritize liquidity, stability of principal, and easy access to your funds, Money Market Funds may be a suitable option.

Tax Considerations: Money Market Fund returns are typically taxable at the federal level. Depending on the type of securities held by the fund, a portion of the income may also be subject to state and local taxes.

Money Market Funds can be a valuable addition to your investment portfolio, providing liquidity and safety for your cash holdings. By understanding their characteristics and how they differ from other low-risk investments, you can make well-informed decisions to achieve your financial goals.

In the next chapter, we'll explore another low-risk investment option: High-Quality Corporate Bonds. Let's proceed to Chapter 33: High-Quality Corporate Bonds.

33: HIGH-QUALITY CORPORATE BONDS

I n this chapter, we'll explore high-quality corporate bonds as a low-risk investment option and how they compare to Treasury Bonds, Certificates of Deposit (CDs), and Money Market Funds. High-quality corporate bonds offer investors the opportunity to earn a higher yield compared to government securities while maintaining a moderate level of risk.

UNDERSTANDING HIGH-QUALITY CORPORATE BONDS

High-quality corporate bonds are debt securities issued by well-established and financially stable corporations. These bonds typically have investment-grade credit ratings, indicating a lower risk of default. Companies issue corporate bonds to raise capital, and investors purchase them to earn interest income.

YIELD AND RISK PROFILE

High-quality corporate bonds generally offer higher yields compared to Treasury Bonds due to the slightly higher risk associated with corporate debt. However, they are still considered low-risk investments, especially when issued by reputable and financially sound companies.

CREDIT RATINGS

Credit rating agencies, such as Standard & Poor's, Moody's, and

Fitch, assign credit ratings to corporate bonds based on the issuer's creditworthiness. Bonds with ratings of AAA, AA, A, or BBB are typically considered investment-grade, while those below BBB are classified as high-yield or speculative-grade bonds, indicating higher risk.

COMPARING CORPORATE BONDS TO OTHER LOW-RISK INVESTMENTS

High-quality corporate bonds offer a middle ground between the low-risk government securities (Treasury Bonds and Treasury Bills) and the slightly higher risk of CDs and Money Market Funds. They can provide a balance of yield and risk for investors seeking stability and predictable income.

MATURITY AND INTEREST PAYMENTS

Corporate bonds have fixed maturities, and interest payments (coupon payments) are typically made semi-annually. At maturity, bondholders receive the face value (par value) of the bond.

BOND PRICES AND INTEREST RATES

The prices of corporate bonds in the secondary market are influenced by changes in interest rates. When interest rates rise, bond prices typically fall, and vice versa. However, if you hold the bond until maturity, fluctuations in market prices may not impact your returns.

DIVERSIFICATION

As with any investment, diversification is essential when investing in corporate bonds. Consider building a portfolio of bonds from various issuers and industries to spread risk.

TAX CONSIDERATIONS

Interest income from corporate bonds is generally taxable at both the federal and state levels. Investors may want to consider tax-efficient strategies, such as holding bonds in tax-advantaged accounts or exploring municipal bonds for tax-free income.

EVALUATING INVESTMENT OBJECTIVES

When considering high-quality corporate bonds, assess your investment objectives, risk tolerance, and time horizon. Corporate bonds may suit investors seeking higher yields than government securities without significantly increasing risk.

PROFESSIONAL ADVICE

If you're uncertain about investing in corporate bonds or need guidance on building a diversified bond portfolio, consult with a financial advisor. A professional can help tailor your bond investments to align with your specific financial goals.

High-quality corporate bonds can be an attractive option for investors seeking a balance between risk and yield. By understanding their credit quality, potential returns, and tax implications, you can make informed decisions to complement your investment strategy.

In the final part of this guide, we'll recap the key points covered throughout the book and discuss the importance of embracing a long-term perspective in your investment journey. Let's proceed to Chapter 34: Embracing a Long-Term Perspective.

PART 15: SOME FINAL THOUGHTS AND FUTURE OUTLOOK

34: EMBRACING A LONG-TERM PERSPECTIVE

I t is important to adopt a long-term perspective when it comes to investing in Treasury Bonds and building a well-structured investment portfolio. A long-term mindset is crucial for achieving your financial goals and navigating the ups and downs of the financial markets.

Understanding the Power of Compounding: Compounding is a powerful concept in investing, where your investment earns returns, and those returns, in turn, generate more returns over time. The longer your money remains invested, the greater the potential for compounding to work in your favor.

Staying Resilient During Market Volatility: Financial markets are subject to fluctuations and volatility, which can be unsettling for investors. By maintaining a long-term perspective, you can better withstand short-term market movements and focus on the overall trajectory of your investments.

Resisting Emotional Decisions: Emotions can influence investment decisions, leading to impulsive actions during periods of market volatility. A long-term perspective helps you avoid making hasty decisions based on fear or greed and stay committed to your investment plan.

Benefiting from Dollar-Cost Averaging: Dollar-cost averaging involves investing a fixed amount regularly over time, regardless of market conditions. This strategy allows you to buy more shares when prices are low and fewer shares when prices are high, potentially reducing the impact of market fluctuations.

Adjusting Your Portfolio Over Time: As your financial goals, risk tolerance, and life circumstances change, it's essential to periodically review and adjust your investment portfolio. Embracing a long-term perspective allows you to make informed changes while staying committed to your overall investment strategy.

Focusing on the Big Picture: Short-term market movements can be distracting, but it's crucial to focus on the big picture and the long-term goals you set for yourself. Investing in Treasury Bonds and other low-risk assets is part of a broader financial plan to secure your financial future.

Maximizing the Benefits of Treasury Bonds: Treasury Bonds are well-suited for long-term investors seeking stability and income. By holding them until maturity, you can lock in the fixed interest rate and ensure a steady stream of income.

Building a Diversified Portfolio: A diversified investment portfolio spreads risk across various asset classes and investments. Including Treasury Bonds and other low-risk assets can provide stability, complementing higher-risk assets like stocks.

Reviewing and Rebalancing: Regularly review your investment portfolio and make adjustments as needed to keep it in line with your financial objectives. Rebalancing helps maintain the desired asset allocation and risk exposure.

Seeking Professional Guidance: If you're unsure about your investment strategy or need assistance in achieving your financial goals, consider consulting with a financial advisor. A professional can provide personalized advice and guidance tailored to your specific needs.

Embracing a long-term perspective is a fundamental aspect of successful investing. By remaining patient, disciplined, and focused on your long-term objectives, you can navigate the complexities of the financial markets and work towards achieving financial security and prosperity.

35: CONCLUSION AND NEXT STEPS

Congratulations! You've reached the end of this comprehensive guide on Treasury Bonds and low-risk investments. We've covered a wide range of topics, from understanding Treasury Bonds and their benefits to exploring various low-risk investment options and strategies. Now, let's recap the key takeaways and outline the next steps in your investment journey.

KEY TAKEAWAYS:

1. **Treasury Bonds:** Treasury Bonds are long-term debt securities issued by the U.S. government, offering stability and safety to investors.

2. **Low-Risk Investments:** Low-risk investments, such as Treasury Bonds, Certificates of Deposit (CDs), Money Market Funds, and high-quality corporate bonds, provide stability and predictable returns.

3. **Diversification:** Diversifying your investment portfolio across various assets can help reduce risk and improve overall performance.

4. **Long-Term Perspective:** Embracing a long-term perspective is essential for successful investing, allowing you to benefit from compounding and weather market volatility.

5. **Rebalancing and Review:** Regularly review and rebalance your portfolio to stay aligned with your financial goals and risk tolerance.

6. **Tax Considerations:** Be mindful of the tax implications of your investments and explore tax-efficient strategies to enhance after-tax returns.

7. **Professional Advice:** If needed, seek guidance from a financial advisor to tailor your investment plan to your unique circumstances.

NEXT STEPS:

1. **Define Your Financial Goals:** Clearly outline your short-term and long-term financial objectives. Identify your investment horizon, income needs, and risk tolerance.

2. **Assess Risk Tolerance:** Understand your willingness and ability to handle fluctuations in the value of your investments.

3. **Build a Diversified Portfolio:** Utilize a mix of low-risk investments, such as Treasury Bonds, CDs, Money Market Funds, and high-quality corporate bonds, to create a well-balanced portfolio.

4. **Determine Asset Allocation:** Allocate your investments across different asset classes based on your financial goals and risk tolerance.

5. **Implement Your Investment Plan:** Start investing according to your strategy, considering factors like time horizon, liquidity needs, and tax considerations.

6. **Stay Informed:** Continue educating yourself about financial markets, economic conditions, and investment strategies. Knowledge empowers you to make informed decisions.

7. **Review and Adjust:** Regularly review your investment portfolio and adjust it as necessary. Rebalance when needed to maintain your desired asset allocation.

8. **Seek Professional Guidance:** If you feel uncertain or overwhelmed, consider consulting with a financial advisor. A pro-

fessional can provide personalized advice and help you navigate complex financial decisions.

Investing is a journey, and it's essential to remain patient and committed to your long-term goals. Stay disciplined, avoid emotional decisions, and keep your focus on the bigger picture. As your financial circumstances change, revisit your investment plan and make adjustments accordingly.

Thank you for reading this guide! I hope it has provided valuable insights and empowered you to make sound investment choices. By applying the knowledge gained here and staying true to your investment plan, you can work towards building a more secure and prosperous financial future. Wishing you all the best in your investment journey.

ABOUT THE AUTHOR

Usiere Uko

Usiere Uko is a Consultant, ILO Certified Trainer, and Business & Finance Author focused on financial independence and entrepreneurship. A former oil and gas engineer turned entrepreneur, he helps individuals and business owners build sustainable income, make smarter financial decisions, and grow resilient businesses.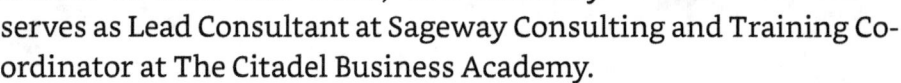

He is a certified Business Development Service Provider (BDSP) and an ILO-certified trainer in SIYB and WIDB, and currently serves as Lead Consultant at Sageway Consulting and Training Coordinator at The Citadel Business Academy.

Usiere writes in a friendly and practical style, making complex financial and business ideas simple, clear, and actionable for everyday readers and entrepreneurs. He is based in Lagos, Nigeria.

BOOKS IN THIS SERIES

SAFE INCOME INVESTING MASTERY

Money Market Investing 101: A Beginner's Guide To Low-Risk Short-Term Investments

Treasury Bill Investing 101: Your Essential Step-By-Step Guide To Building Financial Security

Treasury Notes Investing 101: Step-By-Step Guide And Smart Investor Starter's Handbook

Treasury Bonds Investing 101: A Beginner's Guide To Low-Risk Investment Strategies

Treasury Tips Investing 101: Protect Your Money From Inflation With Government-Backed Securities

BOOKS BY THIS AUTHOR

Practical Steps To Financial Freedom And Independence: Money Management Skills For Beginners

Before You Trade Forex: Things You Need To Know If You Desire To Start Trading Forex Profitably

Before You Invest In Cryptocurrency: A Simple Guide To Understanding The Cryptocurrency Market

101 Common Money Mistakes To Avoid: And How To Fix Them. Book 1: Expenses. Money Management, Making Your Budget Work

How To Avoid Living Under Financial Pressure: A Simple Guide To Getting Back Control Of Your Finances

Financial Independence For Employees: Making Your Job A Stepping Stone To Exiting The Rat Race

And Living Your Dreams

Managing Your Money Post Covid: Financial Management Skills For An Era Of High Inflation And Market Disruption

Retire On Your Own Terms: A Simple Guide To Financially Literate Retirement Planning

Your Ultimate Money Makeover: Manage Your Money Better, Take Control Of Your Finances And Your Life

Teaching Kids Money 101: Simple Parenting Strategies For Raising Financially Literate Kids From Toddler To Teen Years And Beyond

Uncle Ben's Money Lessons: Book I: Do You Want To Work For Money? A Vacation Story With An Adventure Into The World Of Money

Nft Investing 101: A Beginner's Guide To Collectible Digital Assets

Stock Market Investing 101: A Practical Beginners Guide To Online And Offline Stock Trading

Investing In Etfs 101: A Beginner's Guide For Building Wealth With Exchange-Traded Funds

Day Trading 101: A Complete Beginner's Guide To Trading The Markets

Forex Trading 101: A Beginner's Guide And Strategies To Profitable Currency Trading

Options Trading 101: A Beginner's Guide To Trading Stock Options

Futures Trading 101: A Step-By-Step Guide And Strategies For Beginner Traders